CULTURE-MINDED

Six Tools to Transform Organizational
Culture and Empower Humanity

ADRIANA VACCARO

Culture-Minded
Copyright © 2025 Adriana Vaccaro

Cover design by Claudine Mansour Design. Interior design by Michael Beas.

Paperback ISBN: 979-8-9922573-2-8

Published by Thought Leader Academy Publishing
3901 North Kildare Ave
Chicago, IL | 60641

To Nick, Matteo, and Luca,
May you always strive to connect authentically in every relationship.

May you always remember that the quality of your life is a reflection of the moments you choose to create.

Your curiosity, ingenuity, and imagination inspire me daily. This book is a testament to the hope I have for the better world you will help build.

With all my love,
Mom

TABLE OF CONTENTS

"To be yourself in a world that is constantly trying to make you something else is the greatest accomplishment."

—Ralph Waldo Emerson

INTRODUCTION

In 2018, I still held a corporate job. I worked at a staffing firm, and the Vice President of Human Resources position was utterly consuming. Yet, that summer, I found time to take off a Friday and a Monday and go on a short vacation with my son Nick, who was ten years old. We flew to San Juan, Puerto Rico, and stayed at the Ritz Carlton.

I knew the trip was special. After all, it would be the last one that Nick and I took, just the two of us. The following year, I'd get married (today, we're a family of five). Nick and I had always loved to travel, even on the income of a single parent. Exploring our little corner of New England, visiting new places, and seeing the world around us—I never let my budget stop me.

You might be wondering how the Ritz Carlton, a brand synonymous with luxury, fits into that budget. The truth is it didn't—not exactly. Thanks to the points I'd collected traveling for work, we'd been longtime loyal Hilton customers (frankly, also outside of our budget). Knowing what this trip meant in the big scheme of things, in Puerto Rico, it was time to spend some points.

Since that trip, my family has been to many other fabulous destinations (and hotels), but Nick and I agree that

that stay at the Ritz has been our best experience to date. It's not just that the landscape of Puerto Rico is so breathtaking. The attention and level of service we received at the Ritz made the trip so exceptional.

While we spent plenty of time venturing off the property—enjoying the beach, exploring forests and waterfalls, and ambling over the cobblestones of Old San Juan—the team at The Ritz made the experience remarkable with their thoughtfulness, care, support, and love. Yes, love. Every employee, from the gentleman delivering towels to the woman working the kids' entertainment center, chose to go above and beyond for us even before we ever had a chance to ask.

On our second day, Nick and I went to the beach. To our surprise, even though the weather was perfect, there were no other kids on the sand. As we settled into our cabana, unrolling our towels, I mentally prepared myself to be Nick's sole playmate and primary source of entertainment. Wistfully, I thought about the novel inside my beach bag. Then, I began brainstorming activities to keep him engaged.

Suddenly, three young employees approached us, carrying an assortment of toys. They weren't wearing the same uniforms as the front desk staff; these were members of the Kids Club team. The trio had arrived in a Jeep stocked with every imaginable element of beachside fun: a volleyball net, trampoline, boogie boards, snorkeling masks, and even a projector for movie screenings.

At first, I assumed they were simply offering all these items in hopes of earning a tip. Before our trip, a friend had warned me, saying, "You're staying at The Ritz? Bring plenty of cash—they'll expect a tip every twenty minutes."

But my friend was wrong, and so was I. The Kids Club members weren't dropping off anything. They set up the toys and warmly invited Nick to join them—*if* it was okay with Mom.

"Of course," I smiled.

"Don't worry." One of the Kids Club members handed me a menu. "We'll be right here. Why don't you take a moment to relax?"

Soon, Nick was part of their group, playing beside our cabana, and I was perusing the snack offerings (bacalaitos anyone?). I took in the idyllic view that morning and indulged in a much-needed seaside massage. Lying in the cabana, finishing another chapter in my book, I heard Nick's laughter fill the air. I caught snippets of him chattering happily, talking with the Kids Club team about everything from his favorite teachers to Star Wars.

This level of care and attention wasn't limited to our time at the beach. During our time in San Juan, Ritz employees approached us gracefully across the property, asking after Nick and offering possibilities for our entertainment. Without my saying so, they knew my priority was for Nick to have an amazing experience, so they made it their priority, too. They hosted a Star Wars movie marathon, made a cell phone holder with sticks they picked from the beach, and even taught him the choreography of a popular Spanish song at the time, "Despacito." (Luis Fonsi, Daddy Yankee, ft. Justin Bieber)

Our long weekend transformed us into immediate Ritz ambassadors for life. Because I discovered, firsthand, the sort of unparalleled experience that is only possible through the power of culture. During business school, I'd read case studies about the Ritz's legendary customer service; in San Juan, all of that became tangible and real to me. As I encountered the "surprise and delight" that characterizes the Ritz promise, I realized that that promise is made a reality by having Culture-Minded leaders at all levels of the organization.

**

For the last seventeen years, I've had a healthy obsession with the concept of culture: how to design, develop, and sustain effective and intentional cultures. As a culture consultant, my work pulls heavily from validated research in neuroscience and principles of Six Sigma[1], organizational

---

[1] Six Sigma is a data-driven methodology focused on improving processes by identifying and eliminating defects and reducing variations in products or services. It uses statistical tools and structured frameworks, like DMAIC (Define, Measure, Analyze, Improve, Control), to enhance efficiency, quality, and customer satisfaction.

and behavioral psychology frameworks, and my professional experience in the field of Human Resources. This book is the result of that obsession.

While *Culture-Minded* is, first and foremost, a philosophy, it's also a leadership development model. In these pages, you'll discover the Culture-Minded organizational assessment and framework. Elements of that framework have been successfully implemented in organizations of vastly different sizes, ranging from eight to 30,000 employees, in both the profit and nonprofit sectors.

Becoming a culture-centric leader means taking personal responsibility for the environment you create around you. It doesn't matter if five, fifteen, or five thousand employees report to you. You can expect a holistic transformation when you understand, develop, and promote a Culture-Minded organization. You'll see incremental and sustainable improvements in business that, over time, make a big difference in outcomes like employee engagement and revenue. While you're concentrating on culture, profitability, and innovation will naturally improve. Employees who are committed to your purpose will take care of your clients and subsequently improve client retention. Plus, your employees will become fans of your organization, attracting talented candidates to join your culture.

Every chapter of *Culture-Minded* will bring you closer to culture-centric leadership. Each chapter will present practical examples and the testimony of Culture-Minded leaders who have done and are still doing the work that makes organizational culture a competitive advantage. As you follow the program outlined in these pages, you'll be able to self-assess your own leadership style. You'll also familiarize yourself with a practical framework to develop Culture-Minded leaders around you. Finally, you'll learn how to create environments that support growth for everyone involved.

Culture development work can't hurt your organization. In fact, if you're experiencing high turnover or you're wondering why your team seems to be doing the bare minimum, or if politics in your organization ostensibly prevent you from shifting culture, I want to reassure you that this approach will empower you to initiate conversations and influence decision makers to embrace culture work.

Whether you've been culture curious or you've experienced an especially rich (or, for that matter, an especially poor) culture, whether you have the desire to create a positive culture for your organization or just for your team, this book will provide a transformational and tactical plan that concentrates on measurable inputs and outputs. The Culture-Minded organizational assessment allows you to identify the cultural maturity level of your team and lays out a path to evolve to the next sustainable level until you achieve an empowered, continuously improving culture.

I believe culture work is humanistic work, which undoubtedly is also personal development work. As you develop a leadership style that emphasizes the value, dignity, and potential of human beings, you may experience a profound personal transformation. It is with great joy and pride that I invite you to start your Culture-Minded journey.

CHAPTER 1

CULTURE IS ALWAYS PERSONAL

I wasn't always the culture nerd I am today. In fact, at the beginning of my career, I was absolutely convinced that processes were the path to success. By processes, I mean having a set of instructions or standard operating procedures on how to do anything and everything. Onboarding an employee or a client? There's a procedure for that. Sending a contract? There's a protocol for that, too. Closing a deal, asking for a day off, catering a lunch meeting? Process, process, process.

Really, I was a student of the systems-thinking school, which suggests that if you have reliable systems that people can use, in theory, everything should fall into place. Wherever I worked, I concentrated on error rates, consistency, capability analysis, and all the "controllables." Numbers gave me a sense of security—no wonder I fell in love with Six Sigma. A proven simple methodology to improve processes, concentrating on removing errors and causes of variations to create consistently predictable outcomes, Six Sigma is a way to achieve excellence. But there's one factor that you can't really predict:

People.

Initially, this frustrated me. Soon, however, I realized that the people on your team, their level of commitment and skill, their ability to adapt, and their willingness to learn could be correlated to business outcomes even more directly than processes.

People, their messy, human variables, had power. I saw it all while working at a drug-testing laboratory. We had an error-proof operation until an employee decided to drink alcohol on the job and reported the wrong results. Or two technicians fell madly in love, and productivity in their lab sank. Or the Vice President of Business Development went through a divorce and decided to stop selling. Clearly, processes were very important, but people required the most attention.

After shifting the focus from processes to people, I had another major realization. Go ahead and attempt to hire, train, and upskill the most talented, committed employees you can find. Just know that even the most talented, committed employees will leave your organization if you haven't cultivated and sustained an optimized environment.

I'll always believe in the value of having a strategy, developing processes, and acquiring the right talent, but I am absolutely convinced that culture is the most powerful factor in an organization. Frankly, as Peter Drucker said, "Culture eats strategy for breakfast."

From a very early age, I have had a deep sense of pride in my work. I found connection and purpose through contribution. The concept of culture and the fulfillment we can get from our work have been dear to my heart for as long as I can remember. Everything we experience in the workplace is personal.

I was born in Bogotá, the capital of Colombia in South America. Bogotá is a city of nearly eight million, teeming with colleges, libraries, and coffee shops; it's the country's center of business and finance, packed with history—and terrible traffic. In 2005, I moved to Newton, Massachusetts, to attend graduate school and earn a Master of Business Administration. I was twenty-three.

Picturesque and suburban, Newton gives off an intellectual vibe thanks to its proximity to Boston College. There, I worked towards my MBA and learned English; I got by with a job at a cell phone store. After a year, I finally landed a full-time position in my field. I was hired as an Operations Manager for a drug testing laboratory in Southbridge, MA.

Upton State Forest, Hopkinton State Park, Natick Mall—there are only fifty-four miles between Newton and Southbridge. It had only been a year since I had relocated from Bogotá, and I thought this move across the state should be simple. Nothing could've been further from the truth.

Southbridge was a completely different world from both Bogotá and Newton. Although the Quinebaug River goes right through the town, there's nothing picturesque about Southbridge, with its small-town industrial feeling, all old mill buildings and churches. While my education and experience at that point were exclusively in business operations and Human Resources, my new job allowed me to learn about fascinating concepts like liquid chromatography, quantitative drug analysis, the psychology and physiology of substance abuse disorder, and the highly regulated intricacies of laboratory practices. Within eight years, I was part of the executive team.

What I loved the most about that experience was having the opportunity to learn every single job in an organization. I learned to collect urine and blood samples to make sure my procedures were relevant and accurate. I studied national shipping logistics and compared vendors to reduce our costs while keeping a fast turnaround. I used a stopwatch and playfully experimented with different ways to cut waste and create the leanest possible operation. I opened new territories across the country. When I finally achieved that executive position, I could relate to every person in the organization. After all, I knew what it took to do their job. This gave me the leverage to connect authentically. It was my superpower: I could hire, retain, and develop for every single role.

In my role on the executive team, one of my most critical responsibilities was "buffering" the interactions of our

Chief Executive Officer. I embraced this task like I embraced all of my tasks, grateful for the opportunity to learn. The President and Vice President of Business Development didn't give me details about this "buffering," and I didn't ask. They simply said I was to shield the CEO, an intelligent, data-driven leader, from any and all interactions with people.

At the drug testing laboratory, with a great team, we created a culture of continuous improvement, an environment where a lot of employees were promoted from within. Trajectory and lived experience held a lot of weight in how we practiced meritocracy. While this job gave me invaluable experience in business, best practices, and talent management, it also gave me my first exposure to microaggressions or, the term I prefer instead, *accidental humiliations.* It taught me how powerful organizational culture is and the commitment and responsibility that must come from the very top of an organization.

A year before I left the laboratory, I had one of those unforgettable moments. I was hosting our Year in Review meeting with representatives from different territories. I was presenting in our brand-new training room with shiny new technology. I wore a sharp suit, my slide deck was on point, and I was delivering our incredible scores in capability improvement and consistency in the specimen collection process. We'd mastered the art of collecting samples from patients in recovery while preserving their dignity, creating a new way of serving an underestimated group while also achieving great profits. I was so proud of the team, the feedback from clients, and the positive numbers I had to report.

When I think about that meeting now, I see it as a scene from a movie that I might call "The American Dream," where a foreigner's illusions of becoming a contributor in the greatest country are shattered. After my compelling presentation, I passed the microphone to the CEO. His presence alone seemed important; after all, he rarely attended meetings.

He proceeded to repeat my closing line, which was still on the screen, while mocking my Colombian accent. "Our 99.997% compliance rate," he mocked, "is an accomplishment that deserves to be celebrated, just like Ricky Ricardo said."

I sat there, frozen, horrified. The CEO was referring to me, the Chief Operating Officer, the person in charge of all his employees, his second in command, the woman working long days and traveling to represent his company, as Ricky Ricardo, a character from *I Love Lucy*.

Some people in the audience laughed. Others looked at me with sad eyes. I just smiled, blushing, pretending to be unbothered. Sitting in the training room, I felt a pit ache in my stomach. All the satisfaction I'd experienced moments earlier, all the pride I'd taken in my work, and all the kinship I'd felt with my colleagues had vanished. I just wanted the day to be over, and we had four more hours to cover on the agenda.

I know the CEO didn't mean to hurt me. As I said, his mocking falls under the accidental humiliation category. But do you think I wanted to speak in front of him after that? Lack of intent doesn't mean his comment didn't have a negative impact on me. His words made me feel inadequate, ashamed of my identity, and undeserving of a position of power.

Culture-Minded leadership is rooted in our not-always innate ability to practice empathy and understand identity and positionality as we navigate the workforce. Despite the civility sessions I'd led and inspirational culture posters I'd hung, that moment made me realize that one individual could single-handedly tarnish the culture of an organization. We'd trained our teams on empathetic caregiving, emotional intelligence, and purpose-driven leadership, but we hadn't trained the CEO. Now I know we should have. Regardless of the amount of time a CEO spends in an organization, their behavior has an unparalleled significant impact.

The saying goes, we get more of what we tolerate. It's true. Even though it took my boss five years to mock me, after that day, he'd sporadically make fun of me at meetings. It was as though working really hard to prove myself had put me in a new category, an *inner circle* of people who could/should endure his tasteless jokes.

That series of events at the lab made me reflect on what I wanted to do with my life. I've had to work full-time since

I was 18. In fact, I like to work. I like to achieve, contribute, and add value. But that new environment my boss created for me forced me to confront the importance of organizational culture—and its incredible fragility. Culture should be cultivated, nurtured, and protected constantly. Culture-Minded leaders should understand that the closer the bond, the higher the level of respect. (Not the opposite.) While I couldn't leave that job immediately, I knew I wanted to find ways to bully-proof organizational cultures.

Maybe you're asking: What's the big deal?

Maybe you're thinking: She's being too sensitive.

Well, I'm here to tell you that I have endured a fair amount of hardship in my life. My dad passed away unexpectedly when I was six. On top of starting a new life in a foreign country, I became a single mom at a young age in that new country with no support. Work has always provided me with purpose and security, which is one reason I believe workplaces should be safe spaces. How we feel at work affects how we feel about ourselves and our quality of life outside of work. As Bill Marklein says, "Culture is how employees' hearts and stomachs feel about Monday morning on Sunday night."

**

Our brains process comments related to our identity in a very particular way. In this context, I'm referring to the broad concept of identity as the essence of who we are. In the workplace, organizational culture is meant to fulfill our need to belong. When our essence or identity is the object of a joke, we experience exclusion. When a group unites and bonds over something (my accent, in this case), the outsider (the immigrant, in my case) feels excluded. Our desire to belong is powerful, though. It confuses our brains, so in situations like this, we end up smiling. Not because what has happened is funny to us but because we so desperately want to belong.

Regardless of our level of education, experience, power and privilege, such moments are draining. The physiological expression of those emotions (for me, blushing; for others, sweating, laughing, shaking, or even getting an upset stomach) makes them unforgettable. The mental and emotional distress is indisputable. It doesn't matter if you want to tell yourself that you are tough or that what other people think of you is not your problem—I wanted to believe that. It doesn't work. Those microaggressive moments matter.

While microaggressions might seem inconspicuous to those not directly subjected to them, they can lead to profound and lasting damage. In a study published in *Perspectives on Psychological Science*, researchers Lauren Freeman and Heather Stewart examined the impact of microaggressions in the workplace. They found that microaggressions cause three major consequences.

First, they amplify both subtle and overt discrimination. Second, they lead to the unwarranted regulation of individuals' emotional expressions. Finally, microaggressions diminish our capacity to listen attentively and respect others' contributions.

According to Freeman, "Though from the outside, microaggressions can seem small or insignificant, our focus must be on how they impact the lives of the people whose experiences are riddled with them and the damage they do along the way" (2021).

I firmly believe that organizational culture affects our lives outside of work. I have confirmed that through my work and countless interviews, too. The effect of that tiny moment and other moments like that affected my life outside of work. It altered how I felt about myself and even the person I was at home with my family. I stopped speaking Spanish to my toddler son because I didn't want him to have an accent. He doesn't have an accent, but in the process, I kept him from being bilingual, something I regret now. In my next job, I tended to communicate in writing. Subconsciously, I hoped that when people were reading my ideas, they wouldn't do so in an accent.

My work in organizational culture is not only a passion; it's also been healing for me. Now, I speak in large rooms often, and I get paid well to proudly present with an accent. I do this to normalize things that make us different. Stereotypes exist for a reason, and if I fit the stereotype of a Latina immigrant, I want people to have access to the full picture. A Latina immigrant can mean an educated, hard-working, compelling communicator and—why not?—an organizational culture trend-starter. Cheers to more Culture-Minded leaders creating inclusive cultures that dispel stereotypes.

Every exchange with an employee, a user, a customer, or a vendor is an opportunity to demonstrate the belief system of our culture. Remember, this book isn't about the "culture frisbee," massage chairs, or ping pong tables; it isn't about benefits, and it's definitely not about titles. Culture work is about humanity and is ultimately demonstrated through our behavior.

CHAPTER 2

THE SEVEN ORGANIZATIONAL CULTURE COMMANDMENTS

You might be thinking, okay, I'm all in. Give me the framework to become a Culture-Minded leader already. Well, before we get into that, I have to share seven timeless principles of culture.

Mastering these principles will allow you to create a culture that withstands changes in leadership, demographic shifts, acquisitions, and market pressures. After all, as a Culture-Minded leader, you don't just talk about culture; you protect it.

Organizational Culture is a Force.

In 2022, I experienced the culture of Brigham and Women's Hospital. Over the summer, my stepdad came from Bogotá to visit me in Massachusetts. After not feeling well from his type II diabetes, they ran some tests, and overnight, he was diagnosed with stage IV bladder cancer. All of us were in terrible shock. And yet, despite the fear and overwhelm, I couldn't help observing the care he received at BWH was absolutely memorable. Ritz level.

It wasn't just the doctors and the nurses, the phlebotomist, and the medical staff. It was the transporter at the parking lot running to get a wheelchair. It was the receptionist, the person checking him in, and the employees at the gift shop, all of whom seemed to conspire to make our every visit somehow, despite the circumstances, pleasant. The people of BWH demonstrated empathy, care, love, and support through every interaction. They greeted us by our names because we visited so often, showing patience and understanding. My stepdad passed away seven months after his diagnosis. During what was likely the most challenging time of his life, their care and service to him—and to our family—left us forever grateful.

Interestingly enough, while he was getting attention at this hospital, I was hired by a different hospital. I was tasked with hosting focus groups and identifying why residents of the town where the hospital was located preferred to drive between forty-five minutes and three hours to seek services elsewhere. We hosted three sessions to understand the sentiment and emotions about the brand. We had theorized and speculated about perhaps other health facilities having superior technology, accepting a wider variety of health insurance, and many other factors.

None of those differences proved significant. Sadly, our research indicated that patients simply didn't feel welcomed at the hospital. When conducting our focus groups and listening sessions, we heard participants recount negative experiences that they or their loved ones had encountered at this hospital. The challenge wasn't confined to medical care, either; it was the greeters, receptionists, front desk employees, and security personnel. Organizational culture in this case allowed for subpar customer service. The normative behavior of employees providing a first impression was driving away patients in need of care.

As enthusiastically as I was sharing my stepdad's positive experience, the individuals in these focus groups were eagerly steering us away from a bad experience at this other entity. That is the power of culture. Like a magnetic force, it can be strongly appealing or strongly repellant.

Culture Has Dimensions.

Culture is not **what** we do but **how** we do it. Culture is that fluid concept of how we interact with each other in the organization, how we approach the work we do, how we serve our clients, and the impact we have in the community we serve.

There are three basic dimensions of culture.

I. Claim: This is how we **say** we do things. Think about the culture statement and core values on the website, the nice poster hanging in the waiting room, and the promise we *claim* to live up to. Most companies have a decent claim of culture. After all, who would intentionally write a poor claim, right? While it's good to have a claim, that doesn't necessarily mean that you can deliver on it. For many organizations, the claim stays at an aspirational level; it never becomes a reality. Too often, companies write the claim and consider their culture work done. Remember: the claim is not a reality unless you consistently enact it.

II. Infrastructure. Culture requires infrastructure, the policies and procedures you have in place so that you can make your claim tangible. For example, if your claim is to be "*an inclusive workplace where everyone can thrive,*" your infrastructure would include:

- Standard Operating Procedures outlining step by step how you mitigate biases.
- A training plan to ensure you're cultivating capabilities in your employees and leaders around cognizance of biases and equity-driven development for employees.
- Hiring, promoting, and employee development policies remove prototypes of success.

Your infrastructure should be in alignment with your claim. Your infrastructure defines your reality. (If you look at image 1 on page 23, the Claim is a bigger circle than the Infrastructure. The point of the size difference is to represent the gap between the two dimensions.)

III. Norm. The final dimension of culture is the norm, or how your employees actually feel every day while doing their work. I chose the term *norm* for this dimension as it refers to normative behavior. Since we have a fundamental human need to be liked and accepted in the workplace, we tend to adopt the behaviors that are perceived as accepted and expected. The norm is determined by the situational cues we create. In the graph below, Norm is smaller than the Infrastructure and significantly smaller than the Claim. This kind of misalignment arises when culture is treated as a one-dimensional concept rather than a multidimensional approach.

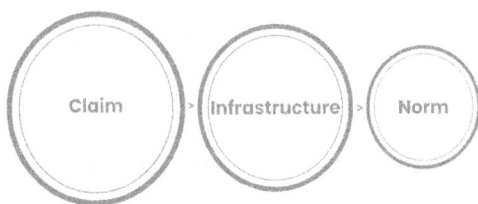

Culture Redesigned™

Image 1

On page 24 (Image 2), I attempt to represent a well-structured culture where the Claim, the Infrastructure, and the Norm are equivalents.

You don't want the claim to be just meaningless words. One of my clients has inclusion as one of their core values. Not only do they display the signage, but they have the infrastructure in place to deliver an inclusive workplace. As a result, the norm, or the employees' experience, is congruent with the aspiration. Can you get there in one day? No. But can you progressively implement strong systems to support your aspiration and ultimately deliver it? Certainly.

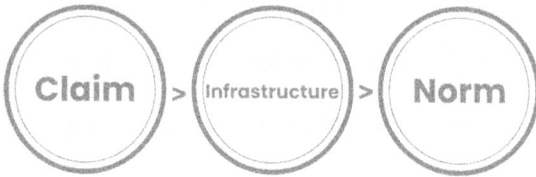

Culture Redesigned™

Image 2

Culture Is Doing.

There is something enchanting about the concept of culture. To me, it is similar to the concept of performance in a "flow state." If you have practiced running, swimming, writing, or painting, you know there is a moment when the motions become effortless. It is the complete focus in an activity leading to enhanced enjoyment and superior performance. In running, when you achieve flow, there is no fatigue or desire to be done; you become one with the act of running itself.

Similarly, in my work as a consultant, I have facilitated countless meetings with leadership teams and business owners where we have talked about the culture they want to create: core values, guiding principles, and philosophical aspirations. I always make a point to avoid letting my clients get swept up in the ideating and romanticizing of the vision. While it feels good to talk about culture, the key to culture development is in the doing.

Think of culture the same way you think about hydration. Imagine if you sat in a room and talked about all the benefits of hydration, the multiple ways to become hydrated, and all that could go wrong if you didn't hydrate. Now, imagine leaving the room without providing anyone with water. Nobody is actually hydrating. Only by turning culture into a consistent practice can you experience its benefits. The challenge comes when we are working with individual identities, and we want to avoid uniformity of practices. When we create a culture of uniformity, we are conditioning people, telling them how to behave. In other words, we're pretty much handing them a mask they can wear so they "fit" the workplace.

Instead, we want to create practices that allow for authentic representation. Our normative standard of behavior has to be clear enough that employees can find outlets to express their identity and their individual core values, to feel aligned while demonstrating the organizational culture. Culture development work is about unity and synchronicity over uniformity.

Core Values Are Overrated.

Core values are important. There's just one big problem: they tend to be underdeveloped, overrated, and underutilized in organizations. For that reason, they lose meaning and relevance.

I can't stress enough that core values—emblazoned on posters, merch, walls, and websites—don't get the job done. Yes, you can have these values, but they won't replace organizational development and culture maturity work to positively evolve an organization.

Our brain learns organizational culture experientially. We don't absorb culture principles by reading the employer's website. We learn culture through the behaviors we observe in others and, more importantly, through the behaviors that get rewarded.

Our beautiful human brain was made for culture! The concept of culture comes from anthropology and the discovery that we need to be part of a tribe or a collective (in modern vocabulary, a culture). We have a fundamental need to belong to a group.

Strangely enough, the same brain that wants to belong is actually hard-wired for exclusion. In their book *The Neuroscience of Inclusion: New Skills for New Times*, Mary E. Casey and Shannon Murphy Robinson discuss how our brain's wiring can lead to exclusionary behaviors (think in-group and out-group) due to inherent biases and survival instincts.

"Our brains categorize people into 'in-groups' and 'out-groups' to conserve energy and simplify social interactions," write Casey and Robinson. "This natural tendency can lead to unintentional exclusion" (2017).

We were designed to protect ourselves. That includes feeling safer around our in-group. Culture development work allows us to create our in-group based on core value alignment and not basic stereotypes. As an example, at my organization, my in-group is not necessarily made of individuals with the same identity I have. My in-group is determined by individuals demonstrating the shared values I have established for the culture of the company. Subsequently, my out-group wouldn't be someone with a different identity but someone who can't engage with the same set of principles.

Culture Is About Reading the Room.

When I present the concept of organizational culture to groups, I always put on the screen an image of a person who is utterly lost. Not necessarily lost in the sense of direction but lost as in looking for the environment to provide guidance. Think of situations like your first day at a job. Or your first day at the High School cafeteria. Culture is that abstract element that allows you to recognize your surroundings.

Organizational culture is what you get from the environment when you "read the room." It's about understanding the unspoken dynamics, emotions, and behaviors that drive interactions and decisions. These moments reveal what truly matters to people beyond policies or mission statements, and they provide a window into the values and priorities that shape the collective environment. It is the "writing on the wall" about the promise and future that is (or isn't) available to you and others at that organization.

As a person who proudly checks many boxes on the EEO-1 report (an employee information report that collects data about gender and race/ethnicity), I always knew how far I and others could get at each particular organization I worked for. (Well, I did work in Human Resources, so that also allowed me to see the inner workings of decision making.) There isn't a more powerful picture than to see how equal work doesn't necessarily mean equal pay. I was privileged to have conversations and observe how decisions were being finalized about who should get a particular job or promotion—and why.

I am not assigning blame. Most of this happens on autopilot, without the intention to discriminate. And yet, at times, organizations develop an idea of what a capable, accomplished, professional, and dedicated employee looks like, usually based on prior experiences and personal identities. We have to be mindful and insightful about how our own personal preferences could be creating those prototypes about talent, intelligence, and ability. What do we do if our ideas are accidentally contributing to the unspoken signals the environment sends about growth?

Just like individuals, organizational cultures can have fixed or growth mindsets. If an organization works on sustaining a growth mindset culture, the environment has the capacity to overwrite individual fixed mindsets. The belief that talent can always be developed is what allows individuals to continue improving and push their own self-imposed limitations. I encourage you to review the work of Mary C. Murphy, particularly *Cultures of Growth*. Murphy writes: "Organizational mindset refers to the shared beliefs about intelligence, talent, and ability that are held by a group of people in an organization" (2024).

Think about your organizational environment: What do team members see around them? What do they experience when they come in as a new hire? How do they feel after a performance review? Are their experiences in alignment with the culture poster?

Culture Work Is Never Done—That's a Good Thing.

Organizational culture is not static. In fact, it's a constantly moving target. As an organization or business matures, so too the culture develops, taking its own form.

In 2018, I began moonlighting as a consultant while continuing to work full-time. Remember that CEO with the Ricky Ricardo joke? Well, I left a job and a company I loved and took an $85K pay cut to join a small start-up that paid me a lot less but treated me a lot better. In order to make up the income difference, I turned to consulting. There was a lot of trial and error, and one of the goals of this book is to help you get down to business in terms of culture and organizational development and skip all the stuff that keeps you circling around an abstract concept.

Organizational culture has to mature and develop. It must not be left on autopilot. Culture, much like sales, is heavily influenced by internal and external factors. While we might have an aspiration of the culture we want, we have to keep a pulse on the people in the organization and also the external environment. Strong, well-developed cultures allow businesses to react to challenges, pivot under pressure, and stay committed to the mission.

You Are Responsible for Culture.

Yes, you! If you are a business owner, if you have a team, if you work in Human Resources, if you go to work, if you work from home, if you are the CEO, if you work in customer service, if you are in IT, if you are the new person in sales, you are responsible for culture.

While everyone in an organization might not be passionate about culture, everyone should understand the personal responsibility they carry in creating, evolving, and sustaining organizational culture.

At my local church one day, I heard Pastor Deryck Frye say, "Culture is how we act, interact, and react."

Every interaction contributes positively or negatively to the collective, which is why we can't simply say HR is working on culture. While there are different levels of direct accountability, understanding personal responsibility and the power of collective action is what makes culture the ultimate competitive advantage. Think about it this way: Other organizations can copy your product or your service. They can even copy your culture statement and your shared values. But nobody can duplicate the experiences, relationships, and intentional efforts of a well-cultivated environment.

CHAPTER 3

MINDING YOUR CULTURE: MEET THE CULTURE-MINDED MODEL–AND THE PATH TO CULTURE-MINDED LEADERSHIP

When I first moved to Massachusetts, we didn't have smartphones. Getting from point A to point B involved printing MapQuest directions at home. If I got lost, which happened often, I had to find a gas station and ask for guidance. I learned during my first year driving in Massachusetts that I get lost a lot. Nineteen years later, I still get lost. (Fortunately, I'm happy to rely on GPS technology, now available to us in multiple forms.) But all those detours and delays have taught me a few crucial things about navigation.

For starters, there are stages of finding your destination after you realize you are lost. There is the moment when you suspect you could be lost: a road looks oddly unfamiliar, and an expected landmark never appears. Then there's a separate moment when you confirm you are lost. The suspicion is verified: You *are* going the wrong way. Next comes figuring out where you are. Finally, you gain the ability to identify the right way to go in order to reach your destination.

Navigating culture development work has similar stages. You need more than an aspiration for your culture; you need more than a general direction, too. You also need to figure out exactly where you are as a leader to effectively identify the path forward.

The Culture-Minded Framework guides you through a comprehensive organizational assessment. This framework supports organizations in understanding where they are in the culture maturity path.

The Culture-Minded Model looks at six capabilities that we consider critical to developing a strong, sustainable culture. We define capability as the ability or capacity of an individual or organization to deliver an outcome. We define competence as how effective we are at each capability. Ultimately, as the capabilities develop, competence improves.

The result? Culture-Minded organizations.

What often happens with culture is that we forget about it. We forget the importance of the intentionality of the environment. We falsely believe that chasing business outcomes is the ultimate destination. When business owners concentrate on getting new clients, finding great people, or improving their product or service and putting culture in the backseat, they get lost. They start driving away from the culture they desire. When we keep culture front and center and develop Culture-Minded Capabilities, we prioritize the right direction for you and your team while also creating an environment that will naturally deliver positive business outcomes and overall business performance.

One of my favorite studies reviews ample empirical research supporting the undeniable connection between organizational culture and business performance. In this 2019 study conducted by J.P. Kotter and J.L. Heskett, organizational culture is shown to be the ultimate enabler of business success. Cultures rooted in clear values report superior business outcomes. That bold statement remains true regardless of industry or company size, and it also holds true in terms of different business outcomes, including revenue, market adaptability, and employee loyalty. While the concept of culture has been diluted and mistakenly reduced to the idea of creating a cozy office vibe, there is concrete evidence from Kotter and Heskett's study that demonstrates how organizations with strong organizational cultures significantly outperformed those with weak cultures in terms of revenue growth, stock price appreciation, and profitability.

As I invite you to mind your culture, I'm also providing you with a validated model to guide your work and support you in achieving and sustaining an Evolving Culture.

The Culture-Minded Model consists of six capabilities:

1. Culture-Minded Leadership

2. Shared Values Alignment

3. Employee Engagement

4. Trust and Collaboration

5. Equity and Belonging

6. Continuous Improvement

The Culture-Minded Organization

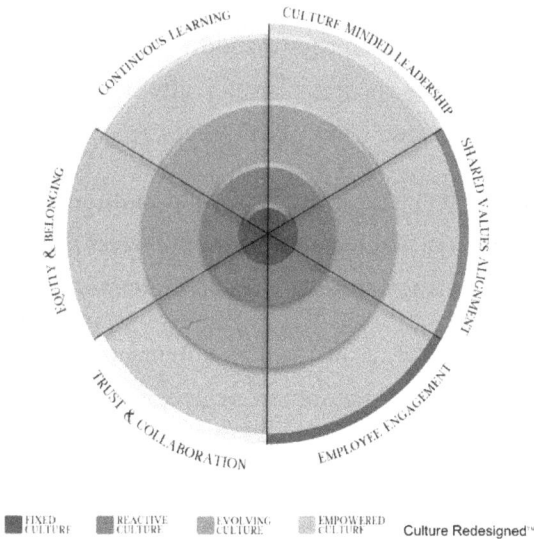

Image 3

The level of competence of each capability will determine your overall Culture Maturity Level. Think of your Culture Maturity Level as the progress you've made on your journey. When I first made that drive between Newton and Southbridge, I knew that when I passed through Worcester, I was roughly halfway. Your Culture Maturity Level gauges where you are and understands what you need to work on to get to your destination of an empowered, continuously improving culture. Culture-Minded organizations can achieve four maturity levels:

Level I. Fixed Culture

If you look at Image 3 on page 35, Fixed Culture is the circle closest to the midpoint (the darkest shade of grey). Fixed cultures are characterized by their lack of attention to the topic of culture. When they do address culture, it is mostly in a reactionary way: after a lawsuit, after the filing of a formal complaint, after a key player leaves, etc.

In fixed cultures, employees have minimal participation in decision making and most employees aren't able to experience collaboration. As a result, innovation can be rare.

Fixed cultures result from an absence of culture development work. If you ignore or neglect your organizational culture, you still have a culture. That culture is fixed.

Obviously, no established business would aspire to a fixed culture. However, for an early or start-up organization, a fixed culture is a natural stage of maturity. As a business goes from its inception team into hiring more employees, it is normal to find the organization in a fixed culture mode. This is part of the development and evolution of a company. That said, you don't want to remain at this stage. It would be like keeping a healthy, developing child from walking and expecting them to thrive by crawling for their entire life.

Level II: Reactive Culture

Reactive Culture is the circle second closest to the midpoint (a slightly paler grey than Fixed Culture – Image 3 on page 35). In a reactive culture, there is at least one Culture-Minded Leader eager to display their cultural commitment. If that is you, perhaps this commitment is what inspired you to read this book. What stymies reactive cultures, however, is the lack of buy-in. Inconsistent company-wide commitment makes it difficult for culture efforts to gain traction.

When I interview employees from organizations at this maturity level, there seems to be an evasion of personal responsibility as it relates to organizational culture. Employees have a common group-think that acknowledges the need for culture improvement while firmly believing it is not their job or responsibility. (Invariably, the job is someone else's.) In reactive cultures, most efforts to improve culture are deployed as short-term fixes. In other words, they have a low probability of long-term sustainability.

In reactive cultures, leaders tend to reference events.

We had a summer outing.

We took the team golfing.

We had a kickoff meeting last January.

While those events in and of themselves may be positive, they obviously don't carry the necessary depth to sustain an environment. Sporadic events create temporary positive atmospheres.

Level III: Evolving Culture

Evolving Culture is the circle third closest to the midpoint (a lighter grey than Reactive Culture). Leaders of evolving cultures consistently communicate and uphold cultural values across their organizations. When an organization reaches this level, it has usually experienced benefits that illuminate the power of culture—for instance, the ability to generate systems thinking and congruent behaviors. Organizations at this level have collaborative frameworks in place, with an emphasis on fostering trust across teams. Most likely, they have employee engagement protocols and multidirectional feedback loops.

It's worth noting that organizations at this level of maturity understand that culture work influences everything in the organization. There isn't resistance to commit time and resources to continue strengthening the power of the environment. At this level, organizations have moved away from a short-lived, sugar-rush, intermittent culture to a higher level of commitment. As a result, they benefit from a widespread sense of belonging and authentic connection.

Level IV: Empowered Culture

The outermost ring on the graph above, Empowered Culture, is the epitome of cultural evolution. In empowered cultures, leaders at all levels cultivate, demonstrate, and uphold organizational culture using a clear set of behaviors and principles. One of the most fascinating effects I have observed in empowered cultures is that team members take ownership of the culture and protect it. If something or someone is out of alignment, multiple truthtellers happily and mindfully intervene. At this level, the personal commitment is just as strong as the collective.

Empowered cultures are a force for opportunities and possibilities. They are characterized by consistently developing people into their next version, creating a collective growth mindset that resonates not only with employees but also with clients, vendors, and external communities.

When our team was designing and validating the assessment, we wanted to ensure that reaching this peak level of cultural maturity wouldn't be the end of the journey for an organization. As such, we've embedded continuous improvement elements for each of the six capabilities. In other words, the process is ongoing. You don't arrive, graduate, or finish. Empowered Cultures are a demonstration of holistic, continuous improvement efforts.

**

While we all create culture collectively, leaders have a special responsibility and obligation to set the direction of that culture. The Culture-Minded Organizational Assessment allows you to see where your organization lands in the maturity model. In the next chapters, I'll share the foundational work relevant to each capability. In the appendixes at the end of the book, you'll find prescriptive-analytical frameworks and templates relevant to your organization's cultural maturity level so that you can confidently keep advancing culture work, certain that you're moving in the right direction.

Where to begin? Start by taking our Quick Culture-Minded Leadership Assessment. By answering the 10 multiple-choice questions, you'll gain an awareness of your Culture-Minded competence as a leader and get proprietary recommendations for furthering your development.

The next level of engagement, our Culture-Minded Organizational Assessment, consists of a 75-statement analytical interview facilitated by one of our team members. It assesses the level of maturity of your organizational culture. To complete this with a representative of Culture Redesigned ™, contact us here:

CHAPTER 4

CULTURE-MINDED LEADERSHIP

Culture-Minded Leadership is the first capability of the Culture-Minded Model.

Ten years ago, I bought tickets to take my eight-year-old son sailing. The trip would be a sunset cruise in Newport, RI. I imagined the calm of being on the boat and the chance to be in the wind on the sea, but mostly, I was excited about the memories I'd make with my son. That summer, we didn't take a vacation. A quick day trip to a neighboring state was all we could manage, and I hoped it would be a rewarding break from the routine.

We showed up at the dock a few minutes early. I wanted this to be a special experience. I wanted my son to get a good seat. A tanned, shirtless, serious-faced man in his fifties brusquely greeted us. This was the boat's captain; more than saltwater, he smelled of cigarettes. As he helped fellow passengers aboard—several couples, a group of girls in their early twenties—I noticed that my son was the only child.

About five minutes into the ride, the captain began to shout.

"Hoist the sails," he yelled in our direction. He locked eyes with me, and after my lack of reaction and confusion, he continued yelling, this time at other passengers. Next to me, there was a gentleman with his fiancé. This man stood up and started moving ropes, loosening belts around the sails. Was he part of the crew? The entire interaction was chaotic and disorienting.

It only got worse. Fifteen minutes later, the captain yelled again, screaming directly at my son and me. "Move to starboard!"

My neighbor and his fiancé moved to the opposite side of the boat. The captain continued yelling at us until my neighbor called from the other side of the boat, "You and the boy need to get over here."

We ran across the narrow deck. At that moment, I thought we were in danger. What had I gotten us into? Then, the gentleman who'd called us over explained that in order for the sails to catch the wind and even out its weight, the passengers needed to come on one side. Like that, I understood.

For the remainder of the boat ride, the captain hollered commands at me, but frankly, I'd stopped listening. My son and I followed what everyone else was doing, and by the end of those long forty-five minutes, I decided that sailing wasn't for me.

Just like many CEOs in the workplace, the captain completed a task and fulfilled a transaction. But did his behavior foster comfort or security, let alone relaxation? No. His behavior exemplified a complete lack of awareness and ownership of the experience he was creating for others.

Five years later, a client invited me on a sailing boat cruise in—you guessed it—Newport, RI. I politely, immediately declined. I wanted to explain why I was so averse to this particular outing, but I didn't. My client pushed. He was hosting a culture summit for his team; I'd be facilitating workshops all day. He saw the cruise as a nice gesture, an enjoyable culmination to the day. Reluctantly, I explained that I found sailing chaotic, stressful, and nerve-wracking. I'd done it once, I admitted, and I didn't really feel like doing it again. My client assured me he knew this captain well and that it would be an unforgettable experience. Dubiously, I conceded.

Prior to boarding the boat, I confessed to my client that I didn't have a grasp of sailing commands. I asked him to let me know if I needed to change seats or move at any point. He looked befuddled, but he assured me that he'd keep me apprised of anything I needed to know.

I sat in the middle of the boat, figuring it would give me the best vantage of what the other passengers were doing. I was determined to be prepared and follow along. Only once the captain started to speak did I realize that all my fear was for nothing. This captain had a friendly, calming demeanor. He was in his sixties, and he wore shorts and a T-shirt. He greeted us politely and told us exactly what we were going to do. Showing us a map, he pointed to our destination, circling the lighthouse we'd visit. He shared a bit of the boat's history and revealed that he'd grown up in Rhode Island; his father used to be a mechanic, and sailboats were his passion.

When we were getting ready to set sail, the captain politely explained that we'd be shifting direction. He asked if we were comfortable and checked in with an individual who was feeling seasick. Throughout the cruise, he continued communicating. He announced when we were reorienting on the water and when we were approaching striking sand dunes. He even recommended good local restaurants.

No one asked me to move once on that sailboat, but I'm confident that if the captain had done so, I would've gone gladly if he'd sent me to the stern or the bow. Unlike my first sailing experience, here, I felt like a part of something greater. That sense of belonging and contribution is what we want to achieve through Culture-Minded Leadership. Because even simple tasks—like moving from one side of the boat to another—can be daunting when you don't understand the reason.

Perhaps it's no surprise that I don't remember the sunset from my first sailing trip. Maybe it was gorgeous, but I wasn't in a good mental space to appreciate the natural beauty. You know where this is going, right? My second experience sailing rewarded me with an absolutely spectacular sunset. I don't attribute it to the weather or the boat. I attribute it to the captain, who was aware of the role he played in crafting the experience for his passengers. Just like sailing, culture work starts with awareness of the climate we create as leaders.

**

What makes a good leader? I've identified three core elements of Culture-Minded Leadership: clarity of vision, transparency of communication, and demonstration of behavior. In other words, show us where we are going, tell us how we are getting there, and demonstrate what you want us to do.

CULTURE MINDED LEADERSHIP TRIAD

Demonstration of Behavior

The leader models the expected behaviors and actions.

Clarity of Vision

The leader provides a clear and inspiring direction for the future.

Transparency of Communication

Open and honest communication fosters trust and understanding

Culture Redesigned ™

CULTURE REDESIGNED

Without Culture-Minded Leadership, an otherwise healthy culture can falter. CEOs have a unique responsibility: by taking ownership for the environment they, and others, create, they steer (or captain) the experiences of all the individuals involved in an organization.

This capability is not exclusively about layers of power and hierarchy. Leadership exists in our ability to influence those around us. An employee doesn't have to be in the C-suite or even a managerial position to negatively influence the environment. Culture-Minded Leadership implies understanding how our actions, inaction, language, and behaviors contribute–positively or negatively–to the collective. It means clearly pointing out the direction in which we are going while addressing behaviors that taint the organization and instructing all levels of management to do the same. Culture-Minded Leaders demonstrate a continuous, proactive approach to nurturing and evolving culture.

**

Seth A. Pitts is the CEO of Bay State Bank, the oldest community bank in Worcester, the second-largest city in New England. I first met Seth when I was moderating a fireside chat for my local chamber of commerce. The two panelists were Seth and Worcester City Manager Eric Batista. It was an honor to be in the middle of these two accomplished individuals, asking questions about their journey. While I had met Eric before and knew the City Manager to be an energetic visionary with a strong appetite for organizational culture health (more about him later), this was my first time interviewing Seth.

Seth is only thirty-six years old but has the calm, collected demeanor of someone much older. At the fireside chat, his words were impactful but in a subtle and mysterious way. He spoke about hardship and hard work as the pillars of his career. He shared the vulnerability of his success. The odds hadn't positioned him for a brilliant future, but consistent hard work paved the way for a career beyond his greatest ambitions. As he put it, the path simply started to form in front of him. Those words resonated with me. After seventeen years in Human Resources, sadly, I don't believe that hard work alone is the way to success. And while meritocracy can be a beautiful concept, it often fails to reward the most vulnerable. In my workplace, I saw how frequently meritocracy was borne of politics and proximity to the CEO.

After the Chamber of Commerce chat, I reached out to Seth. I wanted to learn more about his leadership style.

We met at midday at a local Italian restaurant. We weren't the only table having a business lunch. We sat down, and I got straight to the point. I knew we only had an hour. I reminded Seth of the panel and how he'd attributed his success to working harder than everyone else. I asked if he was still doing that.

"Now that you are a CEO," I said, "are you still working harder than anyone else?"

"I have changed the harmony of hard work," he said, "but the work ethic is the same."

That sentence slowed me down. While his words were consistent with the original message of hard work, something about the words he used—harmony and work ethic—seemed to carry a deeper meaning.

"Leadership is about energy," Seth continued. He talked about the importance of serving those around him by being present and holding space for connection. I could deduce from his words that he was more focused on a relational style than a transactional one.

By conducting a listening tour, Seth realized that his team members had different perceptions of the organization's vision and mission. He met with every single employee and board member, eighty-five people across six locations. The meetings he held and the discussions that resulted inspired Seth. He used those conversations as fuel to write a new strategic plan to refresh and clarify the direction of the organization.

"Vision is where we aspire to be," Seth told me. "If you pull back the arrow, with the right tension on the bow, and the right aim, you should hit that target. Vision is not the arrow, and it is not the bow. It is the target."

Think about how easily an organization can miss the target if it's only aiming for the blue sky beyond the objective. A general idea of the vision won't suffice. *Clarity* of vision is what makes it a collective, effective, and precise target.

That clarity is why Seth is so committed to delivering his vision in such a simple manner. He carefully drafted the vision language, using words that would resonate with his team, allowing them to engage and commit to the target. By communicating the vision in a prescriptive way and creating an environment where people could thrive, values could be more than words on paper but actual shared principles. After all, Seth believes that culture doesn't start at the top and cascades down. Only vision-casting and rhetoric come from the CEO.

"Culture moves through the organization just like electricity moves through a circuit," he told me. "Culture isn't a trickle-down endeavor. If you stop the connection anywhere along the line, the whole system breaks down." [2]

The more we talked, the more I recognized that Seth embodied the concept of Culture-Minded Leadership. He shared his commitment to acting swiftly when unwanted behaviors are observed in a team member and the irreparable damage they can cause. (He gives opportunities for improvement and development, but he won't allow one person to disrupt the work of the whole group.) The CEO's actions are critical to the organization's culture, and so are the actions of everyone else on the team.

**

---

[2] Seth A. Pitts, interview with author, October 15, 2024.

Seth's approach to organizational culture reminded me of the research around signaling theory. Signaling has its original application in biology. If you've ever watched National Geographic and seen a peacock displaying his feathers for mate selection, or a frog changing color as a warning signal of toxicity to predators, you've observed signaling theory in action.

Signaling occurs in leadership and management, too. In leadership, behaviors that demonstrate commitment signal belief in the vision and the future of an organization. But signaling is not only about delivering a message. The critical part of signaling is the fact that the message is credible to the receiver. Just as in biology, where a peacock's display of plumage is stunningly brilliant, there is no hesitation about the veracity of a signal.

How can we deliver that same credibility as leaders? In one of my favorite studies about this biology-rooted behavior, Jacques Hefti and Jonathan Levie apply signaling theory as a medium for entrepreneurial leadership. They write:

> Entrepreneurial leaders must create and successfully cast a vision (the signal) to three different categories of receiver. The first category is the entrepreneurial leader him- or herself. We call this signal transmission 'entrepreneurial self-leadership.' The second category is the team of founders and team members of the organization. This signal transmission is 'leading inside the organization.' The third category is key stakeholders and the in-

stitutional context of the organization. This signal transmission is 'leading beyond the organization.' (Hefti and Levie, 2015)

In the introduction to the study, Hefti and Levie reference Dr. Martin Luther King Jr.'s famous "I Have a Dream" speech. In that 1963 speech, King used the phrase "I have a dream" eight times. That language, and its repetition, signaled his vision for a better future. He believed in the vision first, and he believed it with such conviction that it became the centerpiece of aspiration for many individuals determined to create the necessary momentum to reach the shared destination of racial equity. Imagine how diluted that message would've been if its messenger had been hesitant, inconsistent, and preaching without practicing.

As you advance on your Culture-Minded Journey, you'll naturally become more attuned to the signals and behaviors of those around you; you'll become more observant and analytical, able to swiftly react. In other words, embracing your responsibility for shaping the workplace environment empowers you to become a more intentional, impactful leader.

**

Culture-Minded Reflection

1. Have you cast a clear vision for yourself?

2. Have you cast a clear vision for your organization or team?

3. Have you communicated and signaled that vision and your unwavering commitment and belief?

4. Are you consistently demonstrating through your language, actions, behaviors, and tolerance your commitment to achieving that vision while in alignment with your culture?

CHAPTER 5

SHARED VALUES ALIGNMENT

Shared Values Alignment is the second capability of the Culture-Minded Model.

As the president of Culture Redesigned and a longtime organizational culture consultant, I can detect my clients' shared values—or lack thereof. Even on introductory calls, I can spot their vision for organizational culture well before we start working together. I like to ask questions to understand what is important to them. As much as a client chooses Culture Redesigned, we make sure we can serve them.

As an entrepreneur wanting to maximize my impact, I listen for ways in which my work can support an organization. I pay attention to how the training and culture development my team and I specialize in can improve their current environment. Often, I tell clients, "The fact that you are calling me and wanting to do this work means you do care about people in your organization."

During our introductory call with Silver Oak Retirement, they shared something with me: "We had an issue with a person on the Board. They are no longer with us, but now we have to do some training."

That should have been a red flag. They didn't want to do training or evolve their culture; they had to call me because there was a problem.

After I sent an initial proposal, four people interviewed me individually. Then, two group interviews took place. Months went by; the scope and price kept being reduced to their most minimal expression. But finally, they signed the contract.

I facilitated the first session with my colleague, Dr. Sarai Rivera. Culture Redesigned sessions are crafted carefully to allow employees to practice the concepts we're delivering. We take a playful and experimental approach to learning. In this instance, groups of Silver Oak employees were playing with helium sticks, writing on sticky boards, role-playing, and having deep conversations. We collected feedback via QR code right before the end of the session and received great scores from the participants. As the session ended, Silver Oak employees came up to talk to us, asking for contact information so we could stay connected and share generous feedback. Over and over again, we heard, "This is the best training we've ever had." The present auditing board member stood right there, listening to everything.

Within 10 minutes of leaving Silver Oak, the Chair of the Board called me. I'd just seen her; after all, she'd been at our session and witnessed the warm welcome that Dr. Rivera and I received. Over the phone, she told me that the training could have been better. Dr. Rivera and I looked at each other in disbelief and shock. How could she be saying this, I wondered.

Dr. Rivera has over 30 years of experience as an international orator; she's also an ordained minister. If I failed to read the room, she would've told me—and vice versa. Sadly, we both knew the feedback from the Chair of the Board wasn't honest. It didn't reflect our delivery, and it certainly did not reflect the opinion of our audience.

Our next step was to collect employee engagement data. We told all employees during training that a survey was coming. We ensured anonymity and detailed the protections of the data collection tool. We explained how collecting honest opinions was vital to improving Silver Oak's culture.

In order for surveys to have statistical significance, we need at least 60% of the total population to respond. In the case of Silver Oak, that meant 57 employees. Despite our persistent efforts, we never received more than 21 surveys. Again and again, we reached out to the executive director. We were told they'd offered incentives, gift cards, and more. But the results were the results.

In all my years of consulting, this was the first time that we couldn't use a survey. As a data-driven consulting firm, the data we collect is essential to every aspect of our work;

we collect data, do training and improvements, and collect data again. We believe that numbers tell a very powerful story.

More training sessions followed. You can probably guess what happened after each one: I would get that same disappointed call. Every. Single. Time.

Usually, when I approach the end of a contract, I experience a sense of sadness and also the satisfaction of a job well done. The majority of clients send us referrals. Many write testimonials and stay in touch. Some even become friends. But with Silver Oak, I was eager to be done.

When it was finally time for the last session, the same individual who had called me after every training session told me she wasn't satisfied because we hadn't given her the survey data we had promised. Imagine! Her employees had not completed the survey, and she believed this was our fault.

She didn't own any of the responsibility. She didn't consider that, perhaps, employees were uncomfortable. Maybe they didn't feel safe interacting with a survey. Maybe they feared retaliation. Maybe they sensed the futility, sensing that completing a survey wouldn't change anything.

What was there to tell the Chair of the Board? I said, "We can't make up the data."

The example of Silver Oak Retirement illustrates a pernicious lack of shared values. While the employees were asking us to help them build a culture of respect, inclusion, and empathy, their senior leaders didn't align or couldn't demonstrate those same shared values.

What's ironic is that after we were told we'd failed to deliver data, Silver Oak re-engaged us. It turns out they wanted to re-hire us for more culture development sessions.

No, thank you! As a consulting company, we practice what we teach. Employees, vendors, and customers experience the values (or the lack thereof) at an organization. I knew I wouldn't be practicing Culture-Minded Leadership by accepting more work that could create a negative environment for my team.

**

During my corporate days, I worked at organizations where employees and leaders behaved according to strong, articulated values. I also worked at organizations where the values slapped on the wall had little influence on how anyone behaved.

In 2020, I gifted the book *Start With Why* by Simon Sinek to three leaders of the organization I was working for. Though the organization had a positive culture, it was growing significantly through acquisitions. I knew that unless the purpose and values got clarified and codified, the culture would get diluted, and we'd end up siloed. I also knew that those values couldn't simply be static. They had to be rooted in action. According to Sinek:

> For values or guiding principles to be truly effective, they have to be verbs. It's not 'integrity,' it's 'always do the right thing.' It's not 'innovation.' It's 'look at the problem from a different angle.' Articulating our values as verbs gives us a clear idea—we have a clear idea of how to act in any situation. (Sinek, 2009)

Sinek's simple invitation to write values, including a verb, makes them actionable and prescriptive. Each of us may have a different concept of innovation, but looking at a problem from a different angle is an instruction on how to practice innovation consistently and at all levels.

Note that in the Culture-Minded Framework, we call these *shared* values, not *core* values. Core values are individual and personal. In fact, neuroscience reveals that individual core values activate a network in our brain and help determine what is important to us, how we make decisions, and what stimulates our individual reward and fulfillment system. When a person joins an organization with a defined culture, we want them to find alignment *between* their individual core values and identity and the organization's shared values. We are not conditioning people to be uniform; instead, we're inviting them to be part of our vision while remaining authentic and true to themselves.

When we deliver a set of instructions or make the posters on the wall responsible for culture work, we are communicating at the level of the neocortex.[3] In biology, this level responds to language, analytical, and rational thinking. Sinek argues that when we communicate at the level of purpose, we bypass the neocortex and address the limbic brain, which is responsible for behavior, decisions, trust, loyalty, and fulfillment. Instead of providing a set of principles and mandating their importance, we invite individuals to belong by connecting to our vision and the way (how) we plan to achieve it.

Like the study on signaling, Sinek's book also references the example of Dr. Martin Luther King, Jr. Just as King signaled a credible vision, he also communicated his conviction at the level of purpose in a clear, specific way. If I were to articulate shared values for Dr. King's movement, I would write: Practice nonviolence, engage in acts of service, and believe in fair and equal treatment regardless of differences.

King not only communicated his credible vision, but he also demonstrated his convictions through his behavior. Don't rely on a poster to serve as a motivating factor for your team's desired behavior. Let your consistent demonstration of shared values be what inspires others to contribute and create the connective tissue for a strong culture.

---

[3] The neocortex is utilized in many of the brain's functions, including language, spatial understanding, cognition, and sensory perception.

**

Culture-Minded Reflection

1. Do you have a clear set of shared values?

2. Do they include a verb or prescriptive definition for people to find alignment while still being authentic and true to their individual core values?

3. Have you integrated and operationalized your core values? Are they more than words on a poster?

4. Do you personally embody your organization's shared values through consistent behavior?

CHAPTER 6

EMPLOYEE ENGAGEMENT

The third capability of the Culture-Minded Model is Employee Engagement.

As business owners and people leaders, we must remember that the environment we create in the workplace impacts not only business outcomes but also the lives of employees and their families. That effect can be positive or negative.

The 2024 Gallup State of the Global Workplace Report delineated numerous insights about employee engagement. The saddest and most disruptive of these was the link between employee engagement and mental health. What the State of the Global Workplace Report revealed is that instead of working in spaces where we are communicating at the level of purpose and seeking fulfillment, we are creating environments where employees experience daily loneliness, sadness, anger, worry, and stress. (Gallup, 2024)

How do we create workplaces where employees feel connected and part of a group? How do we craft environments where employees experience a sense of belonging?

We already know we need to communicate a clear, compelling vision and shared values. The next step is to cultivate better relationships.

**

"The quality of our life is determined by the quality of our relationships." I first heard this quote at a Tony Robbins event, and it has never left me. One of the clearest ways of demystifying employee engagement is to ask our team about the quality of the relationships they have with employees, customers, supervisors, and managers. When we show employees that we care about their experience, we allow them to take an active role in shaping culture.

In the Culture-Minded Maturity Model, we look to evolve the concept of employee engagement from that of a once-a-year survey to one of multidirectional commitment and responsibility. This is critical. After all, employees experience physiological reactions to positive and negative experiences every day, in real time. Positive interactions release oxytocin in the brain. This allows us to access the prefrontal cortex and our executive functioning, enabling us to manage our workload and solve problems. Negative interactions generate the opposite brain activity. When the amygdala is activated, we feel in danger, becoming short, irritable, and tending to isolate. Work becomes more difficult.

And yet, too often, employee engagement is measured infrequently. That's the chief complaint I hear from employees: "We fill out a survey every year, and nothing ever changes."

I've heard this from companies with eight employees, companies with thirty thousand employees, and everything in between.

While the statistician in me sees a lot of value in employee engagement surveys, the humanist knows the process doesn't end after sending the survey. Research from the people analytics company Predictive Index reports that it's better not to send a survey than to send one and not address the results.

I often see CEOs getting emotionally attached to the results of an engagement survey and even feeling that the results don't reflect their intentions. As a business owner and training facilitator, I understand those feelings; it's hard not to take feedback personally. But the survey is just the beginning. We recommend that our clients share not only the general results of the survey but also improvement plans and progress on those improvement plans.

On a positive note, surveys not only unveil areas of improvement but also positive areas of the culture that should be protected and maximized. Multiple tools can accomplish this, and while I can't list all of them, I recommend a survey that captures at least four levels of information: Job Alignment, Manager Alignment, Organizational Purpose, and

Employee Sentiment (capturable through open comments/suggestions). These levels allow you to gauge whether your employees enjoy the actual work they are doing, if their direct supervisor or manager is working on their development (and living up to the organization's shared values), and if the organization and leadership are signaling that compelling, credible vision.

One thing I love about data is that you can identify patterns. Data can not only guide but demystify your organizational culture work. Instead of assuming you know where to go, data lets you take a targeted approach to solve the biggest pain points while protecting and maximizing your strengths.

An important note: Choose a data collection tool that allows you to protect the anonymity of the assessment taker and avoids the need for self-identification. In my last two corporate jobs, I was the only woman and person of color in the leadership team. If I got a survey that asked me to self-identify, I knew my boss would know which answer was mine. Tools like The Predictive Index and Qualtrics allow you to load your employee data on the back end and tie it to an email address so that you can run reports by gender, age segment, and job title—without asking employees to self-identify. This may seem like a little detail, but it makes a big difference.

**

What about your managers? Every day, they are shaping culture. Giving a person supervisory responsibilities is a very serious decision. When companies experience rapid growth, this is a common challenge. Amidst the busyness, an employee who is good at selling, recruiting, or writing proposals becomes a people manager. Even if they are only managing one person, this is a tremendous responsibility and one that should not be assigned to someone without the appropriate training, mentoring, and support. At the end of the day, people stay at a job and leave a job because of their manager.

Think about a boss who made a positive difference in your life. Now, think about a boss who made you very unhappy. You can probably recall both easily. Managers are responsible for the Psychosocial Safety Climate (PSC).[4] You can have the best vision and set the most profound set of shared values, but if your managers are creating a negative environment, your employees will demonstrate absenteeism, presentism, lack of commitment, subpar performance, and probably high turnover rates. The opposite is also true: Managers who care, support development, and spend time creating a positive experience have higher retention rates and usually higher team performance.

---

[4] PSC is considered the "cause of the causes" of work stress. It shapes the upstream factors that lead to job demands and resources, which in turn affect workers' psychological health and engagement.

Cultivating leadership capacity at all levels is the best way to ensure employees have positive relationships. Remember that 2024 Gallup State of the Global Workplace Report? Employee engagement affects everything:

- Employee engagement can reduce negative outcomes like absenteeism, turnover, safety, and quality of products or services.
- Employee engagement can improve positive outcomes such as customer engagement, sales productivity, and production.
- Lastly, employee engagement can lead to greater organizational success, affecting productivity, well-being, and organizational citizenship.

**

One of my clients is the American Red Cross. Their mission is front and center in everything they do. While each employee has their own unique job, they see their function as more than a transaction. They see it as a link in a chain of a lifesaving journey. American Red Cross doctors, quality employees, and laboratory technicians alike demonstrate this dedication.

Think of employee engagement as the currency of your culture. You must monitor engagement to be able to realistically have a pulse on your culture. Interestingly, employee engagement, or lack of it, unlike other factors of the model, can be precisely quantified.

To determine exactly how much disengaged employees cost, use this simple formula:

- Cost per Disengaged Employee = Average Annual Salary × 0.34

If you have a percentage of disengagement, you can also use this formula:

- Total Cost of Disengagement = Number of Employees × Percentage of Disengaged Employees × Average Annual Salary × 0.34

Other key performance indicators that you can relate to employee engagement are"

- Turnover Cost = (Separation Costs + Replacement Costs + Training Costs + Lost Productivity Costs)

You can access our calculators here:

Of course, engagement is not only a value add (or loss) for employers. My favorite definition of employee engagement comes from the work of Arnold Bakker and Evangelia Demerouti. Bakker and Demerouti, who developed the

Job-Demands Resources model, define engagement as, "A state in which individuals bring full physical, cognitive, and emotional energy to their work" (2008). In other words, engagement can bring personal joy and fulfillment to individuals who experience this level of passion for the work.

**

Culture-Minded Reflection

1. Do you have a strategy to collect relevant data on employee engagement?
2. Are you able to ensure the anonymity of the data?
3. Are you reporting back to your employees on employee engagement results and plans for improvement?
4. Are you truly developing people managers who are Culture-Minded and fully aware of their responsibilities in shaping the experience of your employees?
5. Do you know the current cost of disengagement?
6. Have you calculated the cost of turnover?

CHAPTER 7

TRUST AND COLLABORATION

The fourth capability of the Culture-Minded Model is Trust and Collaboration.

I've never had a problem being the bearer of the truth. If you're good at Human Resources, both employees and leadership trust you. Really, trust is at the core of your job. It's up to you to be a channel of integrity, conveying information safely from one side to the other. Keeping the greater good as your North Star.

Where I struggled, however, was in being the bearer of partial truths. I remember one incident in which the organization I worked for couldn't pay year-end bonuses. It was up to me to deliver that message to all 399 members of the team. At this organization, my colleagues were more than employees to me—they were people I knew personally, people with lives and families. We were all in this together. Or so I thought. The day before Christmas, the CEO decided to give very generous bonuses to a select group of employees. I was part of that select group.

I felt awful. Suddenly, the message I'd delivered to the team was untruthful. And the situation only grew worse. Word was getting out that some people were receiving bonuses. My boss stood by his decision. He thought it was a great argument to share with me that in prior years (when I didn't get a bonus), other employees did. He kept asking, "Why are you so troubled by this?" The answer was and will always be trust. Employees trusted me.

I didn't want to be part of a lie. I didn't accept my bonus, and shortly after, I left the organization. Frankly, every time I think about this experience, I still get upset. It takes a long time to build trust, but it takes one incident, sometimes even one intention, to lose it. Trust is fragile. (Perhaps that's why it means so much that some of those employees are still in touch with me, even though we haven't worked together in over ten years.)

Part of the fourth capability of the Culture-Minded Model, trust, is a multidimensional concept that can be seen as a principle, a belief, a feeling, and/or an emotion. You can investigate trust through a simple self-assessment (i.e., Do I trust in my own abilities to achieve something?). And while trust is certainly something we cultivate internally, trust is also part of every relationship. Think about five different people in your life. The level of trust you assign to each of them might be slightly or significantly different.

Trust is more than a principle, a feeling, or an emotion for organizations. In his book *The Speed of Trust*, Stephen

Covey defines trust as a multiplier. Its existence (or lack of) affects absolutely everything. High-trust organizations can move faster and at a lower cost. Low-trust organizations respond slower and at a higher cost.

**

In 2018, I was invited to the White House with a group of professionals advocating for positive change in workforce development. I was in a room with people of different backgrounds and from different industries. During a conversation about sick-time tracking, someone used the phrase, "Trust by Verify." This quote was even printed on the back of that individual's business card.

Fast-forward six years, and my not-so-little-boy, the same one who loved Puerto Rico and hated sailing, got his driver's license. He took lessons, practiced day and night, and finally started driving alone. My son and I share our location through the app Life360. One snowy night, he left for a hockey game, and I decided to check his location. I wanted to make sure he arrived safely at the rink.

A banner ad popped up in the app. "You can have access to this driver's speed and awareness 24/7 for $8.99/month," it read.

Suddenly, I remembered the phrase, "Trust but verify." I trusted my son, I thought, but how incredible would it be to know his exact speed and driver awareness at all times? I started listing all the reasons why I might need this verification method. The app would record the location and duration of any stops, any "reckless" behavior over the speed limit, and even the percentage of his cell phone's charge. Under the guise of the app's clever messaging, appealing to my maternal emotions—"Are your loved ones new behind the wheel?"—such flagrant spying on our kids was equated with caring.

Despite being tempted to download the app, something stopped me. Monitoring my son's behavior in this way would be like micromanaging an employee, an employee who I'd purportedly put my belief and faith in. Another quote came to mind, this one from Henry Stimson: "The surest way to make a man untrustworthy is to distrust him and show your distrust." I decided to rely on my son's character and protect the trust we'd built. But don't get me wrong, the temptation was there.

The same temptation to erode trust exists all the time in organizations—thanks to technological advances, dispersed workforces, and remote work. However, giving in to micromanagement rarely rewards the leader or the employee. More often, micromanagement becomes the lazy shortcut to building trust and accountability; it has negative effects on employee morale, and I've watched it lower productivity.

I once met a remote employee of a national insurance company. She had to enter distinct codes to explain being away from her desk. Refilling her water bottle had a unique code, taking a meal break had a unique code, and excusing herself for a bio break had a unique code. Every month, she'd receive statistics, ranking her within her team and the organization as a whole. While I understand that large organizations have to control expenses and monitor productivity, who could work well under such surveillance? This employee couldn't. She'd found ways to game the system. Letting her cat paw the keyboard would keep the activity sensors on while she watched TV. Were her Key Performance Indicators ever questioned? No. (If she was an outstanding producer while watching TV, what were the average members of the team doing?)

During and after the COVID-19 pandemic, I observed how high-trust organizations could adapt, evolve, and survive. Low-trust organizations, on the other hand, struggled to remain afloat. Why is this? It all comes back to trust. Trust gives you the elasticity and flexibility to adapt to internal and external challenges. When you combine high trust with strong Culture-Minded Leadership and shared values alignment, you have a powerful combination for success.

Remember: don't confuse high trust with disregard. I've seen leaders completely disconnected from their team because "they trust them." A Culture-Minded Leader practices accountability, not just delegation, building authentic connections, and remaining visible. Don't let lazy managers claim trust as their excuse for dormant leadership.

This brings us to the second half of the fourth capability: collaboration. Collaboration is the outcome of committed teams with high levels of trust. Without trust, collaboration is superficial, performative, and transactional. With trust, however, a collective objective unites participants; the goal becomes more important than individual credit. In short, collaboration leads to connection, innovation, and collectivism.

In a 2011 study, Ralf Müller, Joana Geraldi, and J. Rodney Turner were able to correlate trust and collaboration with project success. After their publication, multiple successful studies have connected the neurochemical influences of trust and collaboration:

- Oxytocin, known as the trust hormone, facilitates social bonding among team members, which leads to more creativity, effective communication, and faster turnaround times.

- The Amygdala, the part of the brain in charge of screening for threats 24/7, gets a reprieve in situations perceived as high trust, lowering levels of stress and heightening tolerance for risk and innovation.

- Access to the prefrontal cortex, which contributes to cognition and critical decision-making, arises in high-trust collaborative environments. In other words, trust helps us access our better judgment.

According to Roy Y.J. Chua, an assistant professor in the Organizational Behavior Unit at Harvard Business School, collaboration requires the sharing of new ideas. There is a risk involved with sharing something new. After all, these new ideas tend to be in a rough or underdeveloped stage. Taking the risk can mean sounding naive or childish and being ridiculed.

Additionally, if the idea leads to something great, there's the possibility that it can be stolen. Chua's work concludes that only when trust is present do two partners become willing to share new ideas freely, which ultimately leads to major collaboration and breakthroughs. (Blanding, 2012)

Think about your team. Have they considered a better way to do something related to the business? Do they feel trusted enough to share new ideas, even in their nascency, to achieve a breakthrough?

**

Management guru Peter Drucker famously wrote, "Organizations are no longer built on force but on trust." Let's explore three practices that hinder trust and collaboration. But don't worry. I'll also recommend behaviors to counteract those practices.

1. **Regular meetings after the meetings.** Nothing signals a lack of trust more than having a meeting after the initial meeting with a selected few instead of the

whole group. It's surprising how common this practice is.

My recommendation: Decide who should be part of a meeting and why. Have the meeting, make decisions, and end the meeting. If you need to change the composition of the team, do so with transparency by openly sharing the reason for that change and asking for feedback. The practice of making decisions at an after-meeting meeting is diminishing (not to mention borderline insulting). It also discourages teams from collaborating and taking risks. At the individual level, it affects self-esteem and confidence, lowering morale.

2. **Individuals and teams protect "their" information.** For trust and collaboration to flourish, information must be shared intentionally. Otherwise, when results are subpar, other individuals or teams can argue that if they'd known what was going on, they would've steered you in a different direction. This breeds infighting and animosity.

My recommendation: Invite teams to shift their collective thinking from "We share information when strictly necessary" to "We disclose all information by default." This approach to communication allows teams to avoid redundancy, learn from each other's mistakes, and receive value deposits from unexpected sources. It also strengthens the collective sense of purpose and togetherness.

3. **Nothing changes.** This is a major problem. When we work on organizational culture, we work with humans. Human beings are always changing, so naturally, the collective should be changing too. Change allows us to recognize advancements or setbacks in our journey. When I visit a stagnant organization, I often hear statements like: "This is the way things are done here," "We've tried to change things, but it isn't worth it," or the classic "They don't pay me enough to worry about that."

My recommendation: Organizations build trust and collaboration not just by delivering products or services but also by overcoming challenges, developing new solutions, course correcting, and stretching individual and group abilities. The best bonding and team-building exercise we can practice is reflecting on and appreciating all that a team has accomplished together.

The combination of trust and collaboration supports the feeling of psychological safety. When team members feel accepted, respected, and supported, they're more apt to come up with new ideas. This feeling of psychological safety also improves mental health and reduces stress levels.

One of the most popular studies on team effectiveness is Google's Project Aristotle, which started in 2012. They analyzed multiple types of teams, team composition, and working arrangements. The objective was to identify the most critical factors for team success and to discover what made some teams excel over the rest. They identified five factors, with the first one being psychological safety. The other four factors include dependability, structure and clarity, meaning, and impact (Rozovsky, 2015). These five factors are reflected in the Culture-Minded Journey.

The word culture comes from the Latin word "Cultura," which means to cultivate or grow. As you continue on your Culture-Minded Journey, think of trust and collaboration as the sturdy roots that anchor an organization, providing the stability needed for growth and longevity.

**

Culture-Minded Reflection

1. Are there any practices or behaviors that need to be corrected in order to cultivate trust and collaboration?

2. Is there a feeling of psychological safety across teams?

3. Are your people managers practicing accountability or micromanagement?

4. Can you recognize a healthy evolution in the organization as opposed to a stagnant, low-energy environment?

5. Is your organization flexible and able to respond quickly to challenges due to the high-trust environment?

6. Is the fear of being ridiculed a factor keeping employees from sharing new ideas?

CHAPTER 8

EQUITY AND BELONGING

The fifth capability of the Culture-Minded Model is Equity and Belonging.

If you have made it this far, you probably have all your cultural fundamentals ready. Congratulations! Now, it is time for nuanced work. Equity and belonging work goes beyond fundamentals: It's about mindfulness, awareness, and both your desire and your ability to create equitable spaces. Remember: The best way to achieve belonging is through contribution. We can only contribute to the best of our ability if we perceive fairness.

As a culture consultant, even when I'm not expressly working or thinking about organizational culture, I often catch myself thinking about it. The other night, I put on a movie, Tyler Perry's 2024 war drama, The Six Triple Eight. While part of me just wanted to relax, the other part started wondering if the film was going to prove my point about contribution being the best way to achieve belonging.

Organizations can drastically evolve, and that includes the U.S. Military. The Six Triple Eight opened with a quote attributed to civil rights activist and humanitarian Mary McLeod Bethune that completely grabbed me: "We are anxious for you to know that we want to be and insist upon being considered a part of our American democracy, not something apart from it..." Bethune's words lingered on the screen for a moment before most of the text faded, leaving only "a part" and "apart" behind. Notice how similar these words look, yet how vastly different their meanings are.

An equivalent pairing in organizational culture work might be "intentions" and "impact." I hear all about intentions, obviously good intentions, but culture work is concerned with impact. How are team members feeling when they enter a room? What is their experience like if they don't represent the majority? Is the culture of the organization allowing individuals to show up authentically and contribute? Or are we asking certain individuals to mask and embrace the prototype of success we have designed?

Consciously and subconsciously, we all have imagery available in our brains about what is needed to succeed in a team or organization. In The Six Triple Eight, the first all-Black female troop ("The Six Triple Eight") gets deployed to Europe during World War II. There, they're given a special mission. Only for General Halt, a top commander in the military reporting to the US President, a good soldier looks like a man—not a woman and most definitely not a Black woman. Halt had little confidence in the ability, performance, and integrity of The Six Triple Eight, and it was evident in every interaction.

When we interact with others, our expectations have a major influence on our ability to create inclusive spaces. Our subconscious programming affects the way we delegate, promote, motivate, and develop those around us.

What imagery comes to mind when you read these character descriptions?

- Successful attorney
- Young entrepreneur
- Dedicated team leader
- Hardened criminal
- Struggling single mother
- Drug dealer
- Gifted doctor

You could probably describe a person who fits your idea of each of those characters. If you compare your responses with someone else, there's a high probability that your descriptions will match. Is there anything wrong with that? Not really. The problem is not knowing that subconsciously embedded information drives our decisions. Because it is shaped by the media and our socio-economic environments, this imagery serves as the foundation of our worldview. When we interact with different groups, we work on enhancing our mental imagery library, which directly affects the way we think.

In 2014, researchers from Arizona State University conducted a three-year study to identify the consequences of having a criminal record when gaining employment. They also wanted to see if the results would vary by race or ethnicity. Their findings reveal how much work remains to be done in the workplace:

1. Both Black and Hispanic men were less likely to receive a positive response from employers—including a callback or email for an interview or a job offer—compared with white men.

2. Men with criminal records were more likely than women with criminal records to receive a negative response from employers.

3. White men with a criminal record had more positive responses than black men with no criminal record. (Decker et al 2014)

Stigmatized identities are associated with workplace struggles like absenteeism, tardiness, poor performance, and bad relationships with employers and co-workers. When we engage in equity work, we must actively add references to our mental library to dispel stereotypes and interrupt our conscious and unconscious biases.

The pay gap, for example, is a sensitive subject for me. During my corporate years, I not only saw the pay gap clearly, but I also experienced it as a Latina woman. According to the National Partnership for Women & Families, "In 2017, Latina women earned only 53 cents for every dollar earned by white male workers, highlighting substantial income disparities" (2022).

Diversity, Equity, and Inclusion (DEI) work has been frowned upon after the most recent election in the United States. And this is not a DEI book. Regardless of political views, I believe anyone in a position of leadership should have a basic understanding of biases supported not by political parties but by science. When we engage in equity work knowing that we have biases, the challenge can be easily accepted. When we refuse this reality, we might create more harm than good with our positive intentions and lack of positive impact.

Remember: If you have a brain, you have biases.

Bias is "a tendency to respond to a stimulus or make decisions in a particular way that can be systematic or error-prone, often influenced by personal, social, or cultural factors" (CSG Justice Center Staff 2014). Our pre-loaded biases are usually subconscious, meaning that most likely, we don't know our own preferences. I might make a decision thinking that it's rational, completely unaware of the biases playing a role in it.

Project Implicit, hosted by Harvard University, offers a variety of tests that anyone can take to learn about different types of biases. The results of these tests give you a preview of your subconscious. When I took one of the implicit bias tests, I was surprised and embarrassed by the results. By reading this book, you might know that I'm a working wife, a mother, and an immigrant. I consider myself a feminist, but according to the test, subconsciously, I have a strong positive bias toward male leadership figures; specifically, I prefer to work for and with tall Caucasian men. (Insert confused face here.)

While painful, awareness is the first step towards improvement. Understanding the way my subconscious mind could affect my decisions allows me to create data-driven processes. For example, I always use a rubric for interview scoring when I'm making hiring decisions, and I ensure resumes and assessments are blinded to avoid quick judgments on my part.

I also understand how biases can be a factor negatively affecting the future of my organization. Originally from Colombia, I have an accent. I know that there's a strong subconscious negative attitude about consultants with an accent—usually, it's associated with a lack of intelligence. With that awareness, I put effort into building meaningful connections and authentic relationships. This way, people will experience my personality and talents; they won't rely solely (and unknowingly) on their subconscious mind to judge my firm and my work.

As you see, equity work has a particular depth and intentionality. It isn't transactional.

Allowing people to contribute is the greatest strategy for creating access and equity.

Let's return to The Six Triple Eight. The battalion was given the seemingly impossible task of sorting through 17 *million* pieces of mail. Other troops had tried, but they'd all given up and failed. Here's how Commanding Officer Major Adams (played by Kerry Washington) presents the assignment to her troop: "Soldiers, we have been ordered to provide hope. The soldiers have not heard from their loved ones, and their loved ones have not heard from them. When there is no mail, there is low morale" (Perry 2024). Adams was signaling her conviction while also communicating a compelling purpose. She also clearly stated the how: "Unlike some other folks here, we have the most to prove. Now is where you show the proof. This is our mission. And we will not fail" (Perry 2024). For this battalion, the mission was not just one of sort mail; it was a crucial step in bringing soldiers hope while simultaneously proving themselves worthy of their army uniforms.

While I was in corporate environments, I earned respect by making major contributions. Just like the soldiers of The Six Triple Eight, I felt I had to be perfect to prove my worth. I once worked in an office where one white male manager happened to be a close family friend of the owner of the company. This manager would freely nap in the office where two other associates were working. He felt comfortable frequenting the strip club at lunch and coming back smelling like coconut oil with sparkles in his brown hair. If I had done the same or even taken a two-minute cat nap, I am confident I would have been fired. Different people, different standards. Not only did I have to work harder than everyone else to prove my worth, but even more frustrating, I had to put up with the incompetence and lack of care of those with preferential status. That creates resentment and tension in the workplace. Do you think I wanted to belong or be associated with people like that manager? No. Yet, I still had the burden of demonstrating my value to my employer.

**

Belonging is a positive emotion. According to Cornell University's Office of Diversity and Inclusion, "A sense of belonging at work refers to an employee's experience of feeling accepted, included, and valued within their organization, enabling them to bring their authentic selves to the workplace." Have you experienced anything like that? Feeling that you can do more because of your team? Feeling part of a group where everyone together is more than the sum of all individual accomplishments?

Belonging makes you want to be where you are and motivates you to contribute. Belonging is connected to employee engagement and retention. It's also connected to customer retention. When employees feel they belong in an organization, they deliver outstanding products and services. Subsequently, customers also experience that feeling of belonging, which generates brand loyalty.

In his book *Unreasonable Hospitality*, Will Guidara describes what he learned from his mentor, restauranteur Danny Meyers, who revolutionized fine dining in New York:

> The cornerstone of the company culture was a philosophy Danny called Enlighten Hospitality, which upended traditional hierarchies by prioritizing the people who worked there over everything else, including the guest, and the investors. This didn't mean the customer suffered; in fact, the opposite. Danny's big idea was to hire great people, treat them well, and invest deeply in their personal and professional growth, and they would take great care of the customers—which is exactly what they did. (Guidara 2022)

Meyers' hospitality group isn't alone in prioritizing their investment in people and seeing a ripple effect. Outdoor-gear purveyor Patagonia is another example of what creating a sense of belonging can do for client retention. Their strategy for employee engagement concentrates on critical thinking. Patagonia allows employees to share their personal interests and also learn what critical thinking means in their job. Keep in mind: Authenticity + Critical Thinking = Problem solving and resilience.

This is exactly what clients experience when they interact with Patagonia.

There's no silver bullet to achieving equity and belonging, but doing the work is worth it. This isn't just a business strategy that can be quantified and dollarized; it also undergirds a philosophical vision for a better workplace. Wouldn't it be ideal to create spaces where people could show up authentically, unafraid, without anything to prove? Workplaces that support mental health, workplaces aware of how biases can be detrimental, workplaces where people can contribute and find meaning regardless of differences in race, ethnicity, gender, preferences, and socio-economic status?

In their book, *Neuroscience of Inclusion*, Mary E. Casey and Shannon Murphy write about what we can do to consciously expand our go-to people and teach our brains to create new associations. One of their recommendations is to create positive high expectations for those who are not part of our inner circle. Think about your go-to people at work. Do they look like you? By setting high expectations for those who aren't part of that core circle, by communicating with kindness, and by providing ongoing support, we actively foster a sense of belonging and inclusion. When we prioritize the growth and development of individuals who may differ from us, our mindset becomes more adaptable and inclusive. We begin to naturally expect excellence from those beyond our immediate circle.

Equity starts with you as a leader. As you commit to this work, give yourself grace and remember: Building equitable work environments that foster a sense of belonging isn't just beneficial for business—it's essential for humanity.

**

Culture-Minded Reflection:

1. Is promoting equity and belonging a priority for your organization?

2. Is equity a priority for you as a leader?

3. Do pay structures reflect levels of contribution and responsibility?

4. Are leaders intentionally tasked with talent development at all levels?

5. Are employees provided with multiple feedback mechanisms to ensure the workplace environment supports equity, development, and mental health?

6. Have you calculated the cost of employee turnover?

7. Have you calculated the cost of client turnover?

8. Are there opportunities to improve client and employee retention by embracing more equity-driven practices?

CHAPTER 9

CONTINUOUS IMPROVEMENT

The sixth and final capability of the Culture-Minded Model is Continuous Improvement.

Tricia Canavan is the CEO of The Tech Foundry, an IT-focused workforce development organization that prioritizes connecting low to moderate-income individuals with training and opportunities so they can access fully waged jobs in tech. Operating at the intersection of economic and workforce development, The Tech Foundry helps create an equitable and thriving economy for all the people in Massachusetts by increasing talent pipelines at a time when there is a workforce crisis in the Commonwealth.

I first met Tricia about six years ago. In that time, I've seen her evolve her own leadership style and adapt to different environments, but most importantly, I have witnessed her activate the growth and development of those around her. How does she do this? By allowing her teammates to contribute fully.

Tricia exemplifies continuous improvement through Culture-Minded Leadership. She practices a multi-dimensional approach that involves not only her own development and constant search for feedback and improvement but also the practice of curiosity and ingenuity to discover people and process potential for development while maintaining a long-term vision.

I mention Tricia for several reasons. Tricia was the first person to validate my business idea. Don't get me wrong: She wasn't the first person to hear what I wanted to do. She was, however, the first one to see potential in it. I'd shared my idea of starting a consulting practice designing organizational cultures that could deliver equity and continuous improvement simultaneously. To most people, the idea didn't sound attractive or even feasible. Tricia saw potential. If you're an entrepreneur, you might remember the first person who thought you were onto something. That first *yes* is meaningful in so many ways.

Speaking of ways, Tricia is a waymaker. I borrow the term from Tara Jaye Frank's incredible book, *The Waymakers: Clearing the Path to Workplace Equity.* Tricia opens doors, makes introductions, gives chances, and brings people to the room, the table, and the conversation. She is aware of her privilege and wants to use it for the greater good.

Finally, when a company I was working for, Masis Staffing Solutions, was in the process of acquiring her company, United Personnel, Tricia made me feel seen. But it goes deeper than that. Masis had already gone through multiple acquisitions prior to this one. As a company, we had a project plan and all the checklists we considered necessary to complete an acquisition successfully. But the process with Tricia was different.

Tricia had built a very flexible culture, one she wanted to ensure Masis accommodated. From the start, her people-first approach intrigued me. In my role as Vice President of Human Resources, my involvement in prior acquisitions consisted of onboarding employees, communicating benefits, and such. But for this acquisition, I was asked to present everything my department was doing. I had the pleasure of sharing my "HR Matrix," my beloved Excel spreadsheet that detailed all of Masis's people and culture efforts. Tricia and her team visited our office and listened to the HR department! Culture was important to her. I proudly shared about our monthly training, our monthly newsletter, career path structures, yearly slogan competition, quarterly Service Area meetings, compliance rates, and other employee-centered activities. For Valentine's Day, we had employees share why they love their job with #Iheartmasis. Every year, we got together on a walk for the homeless, led by the CEO's wife. Each office could pick different places to volunteer during working hours. Tricia cared about all the programs we had! She took the time to listen to how we managed people and culture; she asked questions. That was the first time a company being acquired wanted to hear from my team and me. I knew then that she was different.

After months of conversations and negotiations, the acquisition finally took place. Tricia went from being the CEO of United Personnel to being Executive Vice President of Corporate Relations and Advocacy at Masis Staffing Solutions. Tricia loved the focus of her new job. She mentioned that the CEO of Masis and his team took the time to find her strengths and carved a position that allowed her to do what she loved while also adding value. She recalls her role as an investment in developing Masis' presence as a corporate citizen. She was able to start Masis' first Diversity, Equity, and Inclusion committee and a VIP corporate relations program in order to engage, recognize, and build stronger relations with loyal clients. In her words: "What do corporate citizens do? They contribute in a way that is good for the industry, good for the organization, and good for society. That involvement never goes in vain. At the heart of that is business success."

In 2022, Tricia was approached by the Board Chair at The Tech Foundry. Of her transition from Masis to her current job, she explains:

> This job allows me to drive equity directly. All the hard-learned lessons from everything I have done in my life: from running my business, leading a small nonprofit, teaching at a community college, teaching English in Mexico, and all the workforce and economic development work from the staffing industry. In many ways, I

can bring all those facets to the table with a direct impact. I feel privileged to have this role and finish my career in service to the community.[5]

Tricia models my belief that the best way to belong is to contribute. More importantly, she is able to create spaces where others can find a sense of belonging by making meaningful contributions. Culture-Minded Leaders are able to activate the powerful and virtuous linkage between continuous improvement, contribution, and belonging. As organizations improve based on employees' contributions, belonging deepens. Simultaneously, employees who feel part of something bigger are empowered to innovate and contribute, creating a self-sustaining cycle.

CULTURE-MINDED SELF SUSTAINING CYCLE

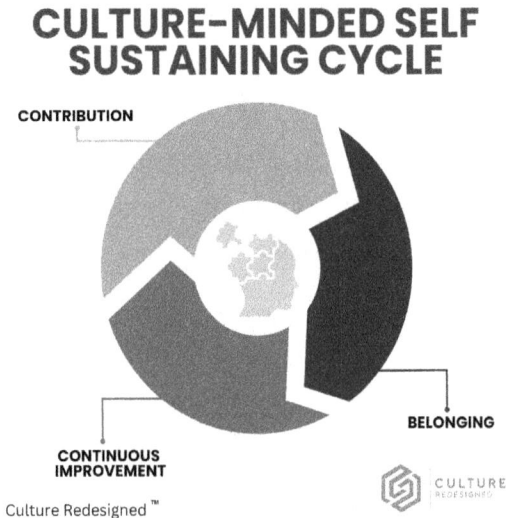

CONTRIBUTION

CONTINUOUS IMPROVEMENT

BELONGING

Culture Redesigned ™

CULTURE REDESIGNED

---

[5] Tricia Canavan, interview with author, January 7, 2025.

Cultures aren't just designed, listed, or announced. Strong organizational cultures are built by the collective practices of the capabilities in the Culture-Minded Model. And the greatest win you can create for your organization is an environment of constant development.

When we intentionally curate workplaces where improvement is natural, we remove the pressure of pretending and replace it with the innate ability we have to become a better version of ourselves. During that process, we support a better version of our team and our deliverables as well. Think about fitness ability, fluency in a second language, musical aptitude, or meditation. Anything that produces significant results must be practiced and cultivated. Cultures of growth and development naturally lead to better products, services, and standards. When we settle, we stop improving. Consider your product or service. If you aren't constantly thinking about its next or best version, your competitors might beat you to it.

In 2018, two researchers at Cranfield University in the UK studied the importance of culture in facilitating an environment of continuous improvement. "The literature has confirmed that continuous improvement (CI) is only successful when there is an appropriate organizational culture" (Almaiman and McLaughlin 2018). Their work emphasizes that a misaligned organizational culture can significantly hinder the success of continuous improvement efforts. Regardless of the strategies or initiatives implemented, meaningful progress is unlikely if the underlying culture does not support or align with the principles of continuous improvement. According to their literature review and research findings, supportive leadership, customer focus, future orientation, and organizational values are vital factors in making continuous improvement a reality. Our Culture-Minded Model embraces those five factors plus equity and trust to make the environment even more resilient.

Another popular subject of research has been the connection between organizational culture and sustainability of continuous improvement whether in healthcare, politics, manufacturing, engineering, nonprofit success, and many others. Studies support that sustainable improvements rely on being firmly rooted in a strong organizational culture. Without this foundation, any advancements are likely to be fleeting and unsustainable (Kaizen Institute).

**

I want to emphasize the importance of data. At the early stages of our partnership, some of my clients have been reluctant to institute Key Performance Indicators (KPI)s. Some believe that indicators aren't always black and white; some are averse to quantifying and measuring. My response is straightforward: measurement creates awareness, and what gets measured tends to improve. If you never step on a scale or check your blood pressure, you might not under-stand the exact extent of an issue, but you'll definitely notice the signs. Just try on those skinny jeans—or try climbing three flights of stairs when the elevator's out of service.

Numbers can describe your current situation. More im-portantly, a lack of numbers doesn't equal a lack of prob-lems. Take, for instance, an organization with a high turno-ver. Even if that organization doesn't calculate the number, the leaders and the team and probably their clients know there's a problem. And that problem comes with costs. It costs money to hire, train, onboard, and offboard employ-ees. It affects team morale, productivity, and the reputation of the organization and its employees. Whether you meas-ure or not, challenges exist. Reliable KPIs allow you to start sailing in the right direction.

As you establish goals across various areas of the organ-ization and make progress toward them, your team will ex-perience a sense of meaningful contribution. KPIs aren't meant to highlight individual success. Instead, they foster a shared sense of purpose and collective achievement.

**

The goal of the Culture-Minded Maturity Model is to achieve Level 4 - Empowered Culture.

At this level, an organization creates level practices for each of the capabilities. Not surprisingly, the most common challenge we see with culture is the feeling that the work is done.

By this point, it should be clear that Culture-Minded organizational work must be consistently sustained. There are many positive effects of this:

1. Your leadership practice will enhance your humanity. You'll not only inspire others to align with your vision and purpose, but you'll also continually refine your communication skills and strengthen your ability to practice empathy.

2. As you develop the practice of your organizational values, you will integrate them into the life of an employee in ways you didn't know were possible. The integration of shared values is a way to strengthen the identity of your culture. It also allows employees to adopt a new positive identity without changing who they are.

3. Employee engagement is probably the easiest practice to develop and measure. With a simple tool like Diagnose by the Predictive Index, you can start tracking employee sentiment and supporting the personalized development of your managers using a data-driven approach (not your subjective judgment). Comprehensive analytics allow you to course correct through small, personalized adjustments.

4. The practice of trust and collaboration will naturally bring higher levels of confidence and accountability.

Once again, follow the guidance of Stephen Covey. As he writes in his book *The Speed of Trust*, "Trust is everything" (2006).

5. The practice of equity is probably the most fragile of all the capabilities. This is what happens with equity. Equity movements often challenge natural systems. You can do the work, but if you don't sustain it, everything defaults to its original setting. I've had many conversations with leaders who have shared how they "fixed" the representation challenges or the pay equity gender gap—only to watch everything revert back to its suboptimal baseline. Practicing equity is difficult. Unless there is a strong commitment from leadership supporting Culture-Minded Policies, KPIs, and rewards systems, sustainability is not often achieved.

6. Culture becomes personal. When you embrace these six capabilities and integrate them into your leading and thinking, you become a Culture-Minded Leader. Welcome to the tribe of constantly improving, human-centric leaders who believe work and contribution are a path to belonging. Remember: Your numbers show you where you are. Get clear on your indicators and keep striving towards improvement.

If you want to connect with a group of Culture-Minded Leaders just like you, join us here:

Now that you've reviewed the six capabilities of the Culture-Minded Model, you probably know where you want to concentrate, where you're already competent, and where you might need some adjusting. This is important work, work that will enable you to effectively leverage yourself as a leader and also propel those around you to contribute to the best of their ability. You know what it takes to develop a competent Culture-Minded Leader.

**

Culture-Minded Reflection:

1. Is there a collective commitment to continuous improvement?

2. Are employees from different departments trained in at least one continuous improvement methodology, like Lean or Six Sigma?

3. Are improvements integrated and sustained consistently over time? Or are improvements temporary and short-lived?

4. Have the teams developed a sense of pride and collective achievement supported by data?

5. Has the organization dismantled prototypes of success?

6. Are talent and ability innate and unchangeable or flexible and ever-evolving?

CHAPTER 10

CHANGE MANAGEMENT

This wouldn't be an organizational culture book without a chapter on change management. And if there's one thing about change we can all agree upon, it's this: Change is hard.

Lately, dinnertime at my house feels a bit...off. Don't get me wrong. There's a meal on the table, with relatively little stress. The atmosphere isn't alarming or chaotic. But, in reality, it could be better. This makes it an ideal time for exploring some change management—in other words, before the needs are critical or urgent.

Here's what it looks like at the dinner table. My seventeen-year-old son is on his phone with one AirPod in. My husband is also on his cell, checking emails and texts. The two toddlers squabble and moan, trying to understand why Goldfish crackers aren't dinner.

It would be easier for me to let them be. All four of them could exist in their parallel universes. If I did that, I could actually have a quiet, harmonious dinner.

Instead, I practice change management. Why? Because I know that meal-time connection matters, and I want to use our weekday dinner times to create memories for our family. So, I tell my husband to please take a break from the phone. (He complies, but not without rolling his eyes and reminding me, "It's work!") I ask my oldest son to lose the AirPod and say Grace. (Which he also agrees to, though first he has to ask, "Why is it always me? Can either of you adults say Grace? What are you going to do when I go to college?") I remind the little kids to stop arguing. Yes, I confess that I love culture so much that we have codified family values: Our 3 G's are Generosity, Growth, and Grace.

Culture-Minded Leadership is about activating change to achieve a better environment. Once I get everyone positioned for change, the conversations start flowing. The oldest will talk about his day. The little ones will say something funny. My husband will miss the point of a joke, and either Nick or I will explain it to him until it is no longer funny. It is, without a doubt, the best part of my day. This is the result of change management in action. Unless someone orchestrates change, things will stay the same and slowly decline. And even though activating change can be difficult, it's infinitely rewarding.

Remember that this distracted dinner-time dynamic emerged; it hadn't always been the norm. In organizations, too, sometimes you look around and find yourself with a new reality. After all, Culture-Minded Leaders are always aware of their surroundings. Much like captaining a ship or piloting an aircraft, those in command must not only accomplish tasks but also take responsibility for the environment in which they operate. As a Culture-Minded Leader, you can spot those challenges and initiate the process of change.

**

I know few people who embody the qualities of a Culture-Minded Leader more than Worcester City Manager Eric D. Batista. Leading New England's second-largest city, he has gracefully navigated countless change management issues. When Batista took office in December 2022, he clearly communicated the shared values that would guide his journey: love, compassion, and integrity. He also crystallized and clearly communicated his vision: Worcester would become the best-run city in the nation.

I met Batista in 2023 when he invited me to facilitate a team development session for his cabinet. This was my first time with the group, and Batista's style came across as dynamic and empowering in a room that seemed homogenously conservative. He opened the meeting by reminding the group of the vision and values and invited them to join him in the transformation he wanted to achieve.

While I was in the process of writing this book, I reached out to Batista's office and requested a meeting. I wanted to ask if the transformation he had initiated eighteen months ago was gaining traction. Batista and his Chief of Staff, Amy Peterson, were gracious enough to meet with me. Through consistent empowered action, they shared, Worcester as an organization was embracing inclusive and equity-driven action. The cultural climate was changing. Batista mentioned his own leadership philosophy. How many people do you know with a personal leadership philosophy? Here's Batista's:

> "Leadership is a gift that must be used wisely to lead others positively, while trusting their abilities to deliver. Throughout my professional experience, this has inspired me to lead by example, not by saying 'go,' but rather 'let's go.' Because of this, I seek to influence individuals by challenging, motivating, and encouraging them to aspire for greater opportunities and success." [6]

The difference between "go" and "let's go" is both subtle and crucial. *Go* implies a directive, an individual being told to go to do something. *Let's go*, on the other hand, suggests a group effort: we're doing something together. *Let's go* is what a team might say in a pre-game huddle. Let's go is about collective, collaborative action and commitment. As such, it evokes an emotional response.

Batista refers to leadership as a gift. His larger mission stems from wanting to contribute to positive change in a world that is full of hatred and division. For him, what prevails is love, compassion, and understanding.

---

[6] Eric Batista, conversation with author, January 8, 2025.

Here are his three suggestions for Culture-Minded Leaders hoping to successfully achieve transformation and change:

1. **Have a trusted inner circle**. Batista relies on his Chief of Staff, Amy Peterson, as well as on his Assistant City Manager, Hung Nguyen. Their feedback and expertise contribute to an educated, well-rounded decision-making process. He considers them accountability partners and expects them to be truth-tellers, objectively pointing out any blind spots he might have.

2. **Empower others.** Batista doesn't act as a dictator or a delegator. As he told me, "I'm not the subject matter expert on everything. Most often, the person bringing you an issue is able to come up with a solution. We have to provide the room and the support for them to formulate that solution." As a leader, it's your job to ask questions and empower your team to execute confidently while knowing that they have your full support. That level of empowerment allows for greater innovation and creativity, says Chief of Staff Peterson. She added: "His leadership is giving his cabinet and division heads a feeling that they have more autonomy to explore new ways of doing things. Changing systems is uncomfortable and requires people to change their ways. If we want

to challenge the status quo, we must first set the tone and almost reshape the way people think."[7]

3. **Take Responsibility.** We're not here to complain about systems or assign blame. In municipal governments, employees will often blame the system. Batista added: "Guess what? We are the system. We work in the system, which means we have the ability to change it. When someone comes complaining about the system, I remind them: You are the system. I am the system. Let's do something about it!"

According to Batista, life is about authentic relationships and about maintaining congruence in behavior across all dimensions of his life. That means he's not one person at work and another person at home with his family. The same philosophy guides all his relationships. His life's work is about service and selfless empathy.

**

But what happens when change management goes awry? After all, approximately 70% of change management efforts fail (Ewenstein, Smith, and Sologar 2015). This staggering failure rate not only has a negative effect on revenue but also contributes to lower employee engagement rates.

When I ask clients about change management challenges, they usually mention employees' reluctance to

---

[7] Amy Peterson, conversation with author, January 8, 2025.

change. When I ask teams why they reject change, they mention poor communication on the leaders' part as the reason for poor adoption rates.

Employees and teams can't effectively buy into efforts that haven't been clearly communicated. The times of "do as I say" are far behind us. The current generation of employees doesn't practice obedience based on rank. In order for an employee to change something about their work, they must understand the rationality of the decision. Ideally, they should also understand the benefits of the proposed change. Culture-Minded Leaders strategically communicate change while empowering employees to take responsibility for the execution of that change.

Change may be hard, but that challenge can lead to incredible growth. While poorly managed change leads to confusion, resistance, and often reversion to old patterns of behavior, well-executed change management is deeply rewarding. It supports the evolution of organizational culture work. The difficulty of change signifies the collective movement outside comfort zones. When change management is done the Culture-Minded way, the side effect is an environment that supports experimentation, learning, and ultimately transformation. Change need not be an obstacle or a hurdle. Rather, it's an opportunity, one directly connected to the evolution of organizational culture maturity work.

**

Becoming a Culture-Minded Leader is a personal exercise in change management. Just as organizations tend to default back to prior behaviors, so do we as individuals exhibit the same strong tendency. Evolving individual leadership style requires shifting foundational habits of behavior. Traditional leadership relies on authority and control. A Culture-Minded style, on the other hand, relies on authentic relationship building to support collaboration based on deep trust. These shifts take effort, and they often slow us down. That's all right. Going from a speed and result orientation to a value-driven approach moves us from the instant gratification cycle and into a deeper discipline of continuous improvement and long-term success.

If this discussion of change management inspires you to adjust your leadership style, these prompting questions will guide your Culture-Minded Transformation:

Self-Awareness

1. How would I define my current leadership style, and how does it impact the culture of my organization?

2. What are my core values as a leader, and how are they reflected in my daily decisions and actions?

3. How do I handle feedback from my team, and what does that reveal about my openness to change?

Understanding Culture

1. What does culture mean to me, and how does it influence my leadership approach?

2. In what ways have I actively shaped or influenced the culture within my team or organization?

3. How well do I understand the diverse needs, values, and perspectives of my team members?

Building Psychological Safety

1. How do I create an environment where my team feels safe to share ideas, concerns, and challenges?

2. Do I regularly seek input from all levels of my organization? If not, why?

3. How do I respond to mistakes or failures within my team? Do I foster learning or assign blame?

Equity

1. How do I ensure that all voices are heard and valued in decision-making processes?

2. What steps have I taken to reduce biases in my leadership and in organizational systems?

3. How am I leveraging diversity within my team to enhance innovation and problem-solving?

Empowering People

1. How do I inspire and empower my team members to take ownership of their roles and responsibilities?

2. What systems or practices have I implemented to support my team's personal and professional growth?

3. How do I balance achieving results with the well-being and engagement of my employees?

Alignment with Vision and Strategy

1. How does my leadership align with the organization's mission, vision, and core values?

2. What practices do I use to ensure the culture is not just aspirational but also operational?

3. How do I model the cultural behaviors I want to see in my team?

Measuring and Reflecting

1. What tools or strategies do I use to assess the culture of my organization, and how often do I revisit them?

2. What is one behavior or mindset I need to unlearn to become a more Culture-Minded leader?

3. Do I have a trusted inner circle to provide me with honest feedback?

CHAPTER 11

ENGAGED PERFORMANCE

My business has gained traction through dedication and hard work. I don't have a network of influential friends dropping referrals left and right. I didn't grow up in a household with an awareness of the entrepreneurial ecosystem. As a team, we face the same challenges your team faces.

Last year, I had a stunning realization. Our team, while small, now exemplifies engaged performance. In fact, we could teach the concept of engaged performance (and we often do), but we didn't experience it from the get-go. It took us several years to become a truly high-performing team.

I remember our first behavioral research project in 2018. At the time, we struggled to recruit participants for the focus groups. We were getting desperate, trying to make something happen. We were unsure how to communicate effectively with the market, let alone with one another. Learning to navigate the dynamics of our work, personalities, and collaboration took its toll. And yet, as we aligned around the purpose of our work, we began to notice and appreciate those moments when one of us elevated the entire team to a new level.

Now, we work as a fully connected interdisciplinary team. Case in point: In 2023, we were retained by a nonprofit organization whose mission centered around providing services for individuals with disabilities and their families. In order to retain their funding, the organization needed to diversify the race and ethnicity of the individuals and families receiving support from them. This new project was very specific. The nonprofit asked us to host six focus groups to document target group sentiment. Our aim was to capture the feelings of individuals with disabilities and their families about the services offered by our client. To be successful, the groups needed to reflect the demographics of the regions our client served. And that's what we did, rapidly. Within a week, we'd put together a project plan. In about ten days, we'd solidified locations. Another week later, we were executing. We achieved full participation in all focus groups and turned around the project on budget and on target.

This picture looks drastically different compared to what we'd been through five years prior. We evolved and developed, and now we collaborate from our zone of genius. Each of us made a significant contribution, yet we all understood that none of it would have been possible alone. We shine as a group. More importantly, in the midst of this project, we all trusted that our other team members would deliver, and they did!

That's the beauty of engaged performance. I know no other company, at least locally, could've promised the timeline and budget we provided. Other teams would need more time and resources to achieve the same outcome. This is the competitive advantage that only engaged performance can provide.

**

There's employee engagement, and there's performance management: Both are important and necessary. However, if you're a Culture-Minded Leader supporting your organization's Empowered-Culture (Level IV), you will reap the benefits of engaged performance. Engaged performance goes beyond the traditional performance management yearly reviews and check-the-box routines.

Traditional performance management focuses on compliance—the ordinary exchange of work in order to take home a paycheck, fit in, be promoted, etc. The motivation is extrinsic. In contrast, engaged performance focuses on intrinsic motivation, alignment with purpose, and continuous growth. Not surprisingly, it requires Culture-Minded Leadership.

Engaged performance isn't only good for organizations. It's good for employees, too. Engaged performance supports mental health and well-being, which translates into fewer hopeless people in the world, fewer broken families, less isolation, and lower suicide rates.

Yes.

Engaged performance is good for humanity.

**

In the State of Massachusetts, the suicide rate of employees of the Massachusetts Department of Correction (MADOC) is alarming.

"Between 2010 and 2015...the average suicide rate for MADOC corrections officers...was approximately 105 per 100,000–at least seven times higher than the national suicide rate (14 per 100,000), and almost 12 times higher than the suicide rate for the state of Massachusetts (nine per 100,000)" (NIJ Staff 2023). These are staggering figures. Equally staggering is the fact that "those officers who personally knew officers who died by suicide [were] significantly more likely to report experiencing psychological distress symptomology themselves" (Frost et al 2021).

This issue is personal for me. During my senior year of high school, one of my classmates, Carol, died by suicide. I remember the day it happened; we were just three months away from graduation. She decided to end her life on a Saturday morning. That event, that loss in such an important year for us, made me realize how fragile human life is. And it haunted me. I kept wondering if there was something I could've done. The forty-four girls in our class saw each other daily: We worked out together, had sleepovers, and shared fashion advice. Carol had been to my house, and I'd been to hers. We had a counselor and a psychologist on campus. I couldn't understand how something like that could've happened. Perhaps we were self-absorbed, so wrapped up in our college plans and graduation parties that we didn't notice how badly she needed us. None of us knew why she did it.

I never forgot Carol. But in 2022, I found myself thinking about her with renewed fervency when one of my former colleagues at the laboratory lost her boyfriend to suicide. He left two young children, a five-year-old soccer player and an eight-year-old princess lover. Even though I hadn't known him well, I saw the devastating aftermath of his choice. I could see how his decision to end his life had left so much pain and loss behind. The questions that had plagued me when Carol passed returned. But now I searched beyond myself: Was there anything *anyone* could've done to prevent this?

All loss is hard, but losing someone to suicide leaves a lasting pain accompanied by additional layers of trauma, guilt, and societal stigma. That's in addition to the agony of grappling with unanswered questions and the excruciating lack of closure.

While I don't claim that engaged performance will prevent suicide, I do believe it can improve the fabric of humanity through its emphasis on positive relationships. Engaged performance actively combats isolation by ensuring everyone feels involved and integral to the team or group's success. More importantly, it provides a deeper sense of purpose. As leaders, we must embrace the responsibility of creating workplaces where teammates can find support, belonging, grounding, and community. We must go beyond communicating basic requirements for the job and allow human connection to become a fundamental driver for well-being, performance, and business success—in that order.

Employees with meaningful connections at work are more resilient. They're better equipped to handle stress. Strong connections subsequently support organizational resilience during economic downturns. No wonder human connection is a critical factor for organizational success. Here are some practical examples:

1. At Zappos, building deep interpersonal relationships aids with employee retention. The online footwear retailer focuses on building trust between employees and managers through frequent one-on-ones and shared experiences outside of work. After all, as TWI (Training Within Industry) reports, "Companies with highly connected employees see up to a 59% lower turnover rate" (Schmidt).

2. Patagonia hires employees who are passionate about outdoor activities and social impact. They even have a civil disobedience policy in case employees want to get together and peacefully protest for the environment. Employees are encouraged to build meaningful connections. Their turnover rate is 4%, the lowest in their industry. And in 2022, the owners took their commitment to climate change to a whole new level. They transferred ownership of the company, valued at $3 billion, to a trust and a nonprofit organization dedicated to fighting for the environment. As the former owner Yvon Chouinard explains, "Hopefully this will influence a new form of capitalism that doesn't end up with a few rich people and a bunch of poor people" (Gelles 2022).

3. HubSpot implemented their HEART culture (Humble, Empathetic, Adaptable, Remarkable, Transparent) as a foundation to support meaningful human connection.

"92% of HubSpot employees report feeling proud to work for the company" ("HubSpot," 2024).

In the words of Aristotle, "Pleasure in the job puts perfection in the work." Throughout the Culture-Minded Journey, remember: We are human first. Let's commit to the creation and sustainability of workplaces that fulfill, even partially, our search for meaning and joy. Outstanding business performance will come naturally from that human-centric approach.

**

In May 2023, US Surgeon General Dr. Vivek H. Murthy initiated a campaign to address loneliness. Murthy urged: "Given the significant health consequences of loneliness and isolation, we must prioritize building social connections the same way we have prioritized other critical public health issues such as tobacco, obesity, and substance use disorders. Together, we can build a country that's healthier, more resilient, less lonely, and more connected" (2023). Isn't fostering a healthy workplace culture a great solution to this problem? While we must address the challenges of children and young adults, the workplace is an outlet to address this concerning issue in the workforce.

Two-thirds of workers (67%) said that they feel lonely at work some or all of the time.

Authentic connections at work not only lead to a healthier lifestyle (one that's less lonely) but also allow us to get oxytocin from positive brain activity, which is obtained when we're contributing to a greater cause.

Let's talk about what it takes to create authentic connections the Culture-Minded way.

As an immigrant and a person who moved to a different country without any family, I have created lasting relationships through my development and the development of those around me. I remember a CEO who gave me an opportunity to speak in public in front of a large audience when public speaking wasn't my strength. He gave me a chance to prove myself and simultaneously helped me see how important developing this skill was for my career. He invited me to speak imperfectly and supported my journey as I turned fear into a strength. No matter how many years go by, I will always remember that first stage—not as a place of failure but as a stepping stone. I remember that CEO's words, too: "You won't get as far as you want if you are unable to speak confidently in front of different audiences." Now, I share those same words with individuals who I want to motivate into imperfect action. My authentic connection with him allowed me to learn a new skill and to feel worthy of that skill. He didn't buy into my own limiting beliefs— he broke through them. That experience equipped me with the ability to do the same for others.

Have you ever been asked that cliche question: If you could display a message on a billboard, what would it be? For me, it would be: "1:1 Meetings. Where connection starts, trust deepens, and greatness begins." As we support the development of others, we continue developing ourselves. More importantly, we nourish lasting relationships.

The universe gifted us with the wonder of one-on-one meetings. If only we knew better what to do with them. We want to rely on systems and software and kudos on a platform, but I invite you to rediscover the power of a meaningful one-on-one meeting. Creating the space for them shows the person you're meeting with that they matter. Also, they humanize work. While I believe in metrics, one-on-one meetings allow us to connect fully as individuals. When I say fully, I mean as people with identities that exist beyond the tasks or deadlines that we're responsible for. These types of exchanges are integral to building culture. After all, one-on-one meetings give us an outlet to make those value deposits in relationships while affording us an opportunity to model the behaviors we want to see in others. They're vital in ensuring alignment with vision and purpose. And, if you hold one-on-one meetings regularly, you normalize providing enriching feedback to your team, creating that atmosphere of continuous improvement. Feedback is a powerful tool that supports engaged performance. It's what turns that essential imperfect first step into a discipline and eventually a competence.

Empowered cultures are characterized by having structured feedback mechanisms, not with the intention to script every interaction, but with the purpose of giving individuals the chance to support each other through relevant, timely, and well-communicated input. Structured Feedback allows you to practice radical candor. In the words of Kim Scott, "Radical Candor is what happens when you care personally and challenge directly" (2017). This approach to feedback requires leaders to have the desire and ability to constantly evaluate their team and support their transformation. It also requires them to have the courage to be truth tellers and the patience to listen actively in order to support the growth of the organization. Feedback, when provided with kindness and respect, is unforgettable.

I have a public speaking coach, Maritza. Last summer, I was the keynote speaker for the leadership summit of a global nonprofit organization. I asked Maritza if she would give me some feedback on my slides and presentation. I was excited about the material I'd put together. This was right before the 2024 US presidential elections. Maritza loved the slides and the approach to the content, and she also shone a light on a potential problem: I used the term "great leadership" repeatedly. Regardless of my political views or the views of the audience, the language I was using was triggering "election thoughts," which tend to be confrontational and divisive. During his 2024 presidential campaign, Donald Trump used the slogan "Make America Great Again!" Just by replacing the adjective, I could achieve a more apolitical message. If it wasn't for her feedback, I wouldn't have had the opportunity to correct it. That talk was the highlight of my work last year. So many people came to me after the event and even the next day in the hotel complimenting my presentation. Small adjustments can make big differences.

**

As a Culture-Minded Leader, it's your responsibility to respectfully and directly address a mismatch between confidence and competence. This is one of the most common challenges that team leaders encounter. A confidence-competence mismatch usually shows up in a leader who lacks courage or has some level of nepotism or preferential treatment.

Have you ever worked with a friend or family member? I once worked with a friend who was lazy. She was a good friend, but her work performance wasn't even average. Sadly, at that time in my life (in my early twenties), I didn't have the courage to tell her. Have you been in a room with a person who thinks their job is excellent while everyone else feels differently? Let's build workplaces where employees, regardless of their connections or lack thereof, can achieve development. That will not only solve the loneliness problem, but it will also support continuous improvement for humankind and for businesses.

Engaged performance breaks the paradigm of leading with your strengths. That theory can be limiting! I often hear the saying, "Stick to your strengths." I disagree. If we stick to our strengths, we don't stretch or develop or improve. We won't get to experience what it feels like to surprise not only those around us but ourselves. For me, just the thought of writing a book was a major stretch. I'm not a writer. English isn't my first language, and my love language is numbers, not words. However, this experience has allowed me to grow and develop. To wake up new connections and possibilities in my brain. To connect and build relationships with writing experts who weren't in my sphere prior to this book.

Dr. Martin Luther King Jr., known today as one of the most powerful and inspiring public speakers in history, wasn't always confident in his oratorical abilities. As a young boy, he faced challenges with public speaking and shied away from the spotlight. However, through perseverance, education, and practice, he developed his skills, transforming into the eloquent orator who led a movement, inspired millions, and left an enduring legacy. His journey serves as a powerful reminder that mastery often begins with humble beginnings and a willingness to grow.

When we grow, we often reach new heights. When my oldest son was a sophomore in high school, he was cut from the ice hockey team. As a Freshman, he'd played Junior Varsity, which subconsciously gave us all the idea that he was going to make the team. Well, tryouts came and went, the roster got posted, and surprise, surprise: He was not on the team. As a mom, I wanted to fix it, but what could I do? He attends an all-boy school, and the shock of not being on the team was drastic. He has played ice hockey since he was little. It has been a constant in our lives. I couldn't believe that he was done with it.

He had three options: He could transfer high schools, which he didn't want to do; he could play for a private club, which he also didn't want to do; or he could try out for a higher level team. He went with the last option, five grueling nights of tryouts with kids from across the country. I reminded him to view it as a learning experience. Even if he didn't make the team, trying out was a lesson in itself.

Well... he made it! He made a better team than the one he was cut from. How's that for irony and pushing the upper limits? When employees are fully engaged, they bring their skills *and* their passion, creativity, and commitment to their work. This level of engagement fosters resilience and motivation, enabling individuals and teams to push beyond perceived limits and achieve exceptional results. By cultivating a culture that values purpose, recognition, and continuous growth, organizations can empower their workforce to embrace challenges, innovate, and consistently reach higher levels of performance. Engaged performance isn't just about meeting goals—it's about redefining what's possible.

CHAPTER 12

CULTURE IS DOING: CULTURE-MINDED LEADERSHIP IN PRACTICE

I said it before: Culture work is never done, and that's a good thing. It's exciting to be in the process of continuously developing an empowered culture for your organization.

Since 2022, I've had the privilege of working for the American Red Cross. The Biomed division has done culture work, and they've invited me to facilitate sessions and workshops on the importance of culture and, more specifically, culture sustainability. Something I admire about the American Red Cross is their commitment to "one mission, one team." There are so many divisions: supply chain, service delivery, laboratory services, etc. They have operations in numerous territories, and they have a global responsibility to respond to most humanitarian crises, and yet they make time to bring people together to strategize about developing their culture. Think about the American Red Cross the next time you believe there is no time for cultural work. This organization knows the mission, the vision, and obviously the culture they want to continuously cultivate. They also know that they will never be done, and that is exactly how they keep their culture alive and agile. They continuously evolve while staying absolutely committed to their ultimate mission of saving lives.

As Culture-Minded Leaders, we must work on our personal competency in the six capabilities of the model. The most inspiring leaders I have met in my career are characterized by their relentless curiosity and effort to grow. By default, they become catalysts for the development of those around them. Culture-Minded Leaders can't be ignored. They stand out. They are infectious and inspiring.

Yes. They obviously carry fears, have bad days, and hit walls, but they continue to act even when in fear. Fear and Culture-Minded action are not mutually exclusive.

Will the Culture-Minded Leadership Journey be perfect? Of course not. It can be frustrating to see an employee leave an organization deeply committed to building a strong culture, especially for something as simple as being five minutes closer to home. Yet, my passion for humanity always outweighs the disappointment, reminding me to respect their personal needs and choices. I am convinced that healthy workplace cultures have a positive trickling effect. That effect goes beyond employees and revenues and into families, society, and humanity.

We have designed a comprehensive, facilitated organizational culture assessment to guide the work for our clients. We also offer descriptions of the four Culture-Minded Maturity levels. Review the information or, better yet, reach out for a comprehensive assessment. Either way, we have recommendations to support your culture's maturation and growth.

Moving up from Fixed Culture (Level 1) to Reactive Culture (Level II)

Most organizations I work with are Level I. They have a Fixed Culture, which is characterized by having a cultural aspiration (but not a yet tangible culture). The move to a Reactive Culture requires a willingness to let go of "this is how we've always done it" thinking that characterizes a Fixed Culture. During this transition, Culture-Minded Leaders must demonstrate openness to change, acknowledging when past approaches no longer serve the organization.

The most rewarding part of this transition is laying the foundation for advancing to a continuous Improvement Culture and higher levels of maturity. During this process, we support clients by developing a Culture Blueprint. Like any blueprint, this is a set of instructions. It translates shared values into desired behaviors that are embedded into personal interactions.

You can find a more information about our model on Appendix 1, and step by step instructions to create a culture blueprint on Appendix 2.

Moving up from Reactive Culture (Level II) to Evolving Culture (Level III)

The greatest benefit of an Evolving Culture is the ability to anticipate challenges instead of merely reacting to them. Evolving Cultures have structured feedback loops and channels to facilitate cross-collaboration and communication across teams and divisions. Culture-Minded Leaders encourage teams to consistently refine processes, services, and behaviors to remain relevant and competitive.

To support organizations in this transition, I focus on normalizing constructive conflict. This is possible through the creation of analytical frameworks in alignment with shared values to encourage courageous conversations and support development while maintaining psychological safety and trust.

You can find a Trust Mapping exercise on Appendix 3.

Moving up from Evolving Culture (Level III) to Empowered Culture (Level IV)

In an Empowered Culture, continuous improvement is built into all capabilities. This creates a dynamic, flexible environment. Probably the greatest advantage of Evolving Cultures is the ability to embrace and sustain change. Instead of resistance, we get absorption of new ideas, integration of change, and expansion of collective talents.

The presence of three elements indicates an Empowered Culture: accountability, trust, and psychological safety. These elements affect everything in the organization. I like to call this the Culture Sustainability Three-Legged Stool. While these three elements are discrete, they are highly connected. In a way, you can't have one without having the other two. Subsequently, if one gets shaky, the other two are affected. For example, think about psychological safety, our level of comfort being vulnerable in the workplace. We can't consider that if we don't trust the people around us. If you can't trust them, chances are accountability is low.

The three-legged stool creates a unique dynamic, one that many refer to as a "dream team." Dream teams can navigate challenges, setbacks, and changes with flexibility and determination. They learn from failures and use them as opportunities for growth.

See Appendix 4.

CULTURE SUSTAINABILITY THREE LEGGED STOOL

Accountability

Trust

Culture Redesigned ™

Psychological Safety

CULTURE REDESIGNED

AFTERWORD

It's taken me twelve chapters to realize that *Culture-Minded* didn't come solely from research, consulting experience, and a career in Human Resources. It comes from a deeper desire to challenge the notion of fitting in. Perhaps it is my attempt to encourage myself and those around me to embrace and even appreciate those moments when we feel like misfits. The world needs more of our authenticity, not less.

Culture-Minded comes from a very personal journey, one that has been marked by moments of great loss and also moments of deep connection. When I was just six years old, my father suddenly and tragically passed away. In an instant, I became acutely aware of how different my new reality was from the norm. The experience gave me an intimate understanding of mortality and abandonment. It was simply the new reality I had to navigate. Seeing my mother feeling a particular type of anguish and, at the same time, becoming a single parent of three kids without an income was hard. I watched my older brother and sister struggle with their need to "help" me because I was significantly younger. It was difficult for me to accept my new identity, too. A person I loved was gone, and a part of me was gone, too. I couldn't sit at the piano anymore: after all, I'd only played piano with my dad.

From that moment on, I became keenly aware of those environments where I didn't quite feel like I belonged, like the father-daughter dance at my all-girls Catholic school. That sense of otherness would return through the years, whether it was being the only student working full-time while attending college or the only member with an accent at a board meeting or the only single mother on Parent Teacher Association (PTA) night. I can say with levity that I am a chronic misfit.

Yet those moments instilled in me a greater sense of empathy. Those experiences gave me the awareness and ability to create spaces with one goal: avoiding giving someone else that same othered feeling I was so familiar with. My story also gave me the strength to find belonging in unexpected places, to form relationships that transcended titles and time, and to embrace the beauty of being a little or a lot different. My journey has given me one of the greatest gifts— the courage to be my true self in any room I enter—because I know that when others experience my authenticity, they have the courage to be their own authentic selves.

Throughout my career, I've had the privilege to work for very inspiring people. Even through transient interactions, we can learn a lot from each other. I have seen that even in most fleeting moments, there is an opportunity to connect meaningfully, to learn, and to leave each other better than we found one another. Culture isn't static. It is alive and breathing, and it is our collective creation.

Culture-Minded to me, is more than a leadership philosophy. It goes beyond business performance and profits. The Culture-Minded Journey is empowering. It's about shifting from positive intention to positive impact. It is about choosing to lead with awareness. It allows you to activate the change that you most want to see but nobody dares to start. Organizational cultures shape not only our workplaces but also our decisions, interactions, relationships, and ultimately, our lives.

My goal is that you feel inspired, empowered, and well-equipped to start and/or continue your Culture-Minded Journey. It won't happen overnight, but it will happen, and you don't have to do it alone. If this journey is important to you, please reach out to me.

So, thank you. Thank you for picking up this book and embarking on this journey with me. Your Culture-Minded approach has the power to inspire change far beyond what you can see today. Like everything else in life, it starts with a decision. My hope is that together we start a collective butterfly effect of Culture-Minded Leaders.

One last request: The next time you are with someone, please put the phone down. Be present. Be the person who listens to understand (not to judge or just reply). Mean what you are saying and don't just agree because it's polite.

Can you imagine the collective transformation we could achieve if more people thought the Culture-Minded way? Not only would we have better products and services, but we would also have better mental health, less loneliness, fewer broken families, less misery, and less destruction. Collectively, we could make the world a better place, one workplace culture at a time.

Always,
Adriana

1 Thessalonians 5:11

"Therefore encourage one another and build each other up, just as in fact you are doing."

APPENDICES

APPENDIX 1

The Culture-Minded Organization: Our Framework in Review

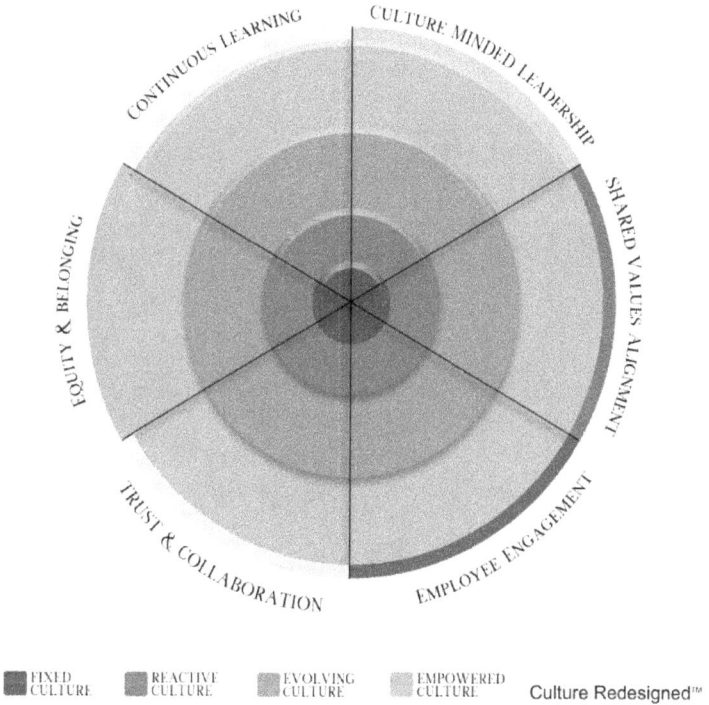

CONTINUOUS LEARNING · CULTURE MINDED LEADERSHIP · SHARED VALUES ALIGNMENT · EMPLOYEE ENGAGEMENT · TRUST & COLLABORATION · EQUITY & BELONGING

FIXED CULTURE   REACTIVE CULTURE   EVOLVING CULTURE   EMPOWERED CULTURE   Culture Redesigned™

CULTURE MATURITY MODEL

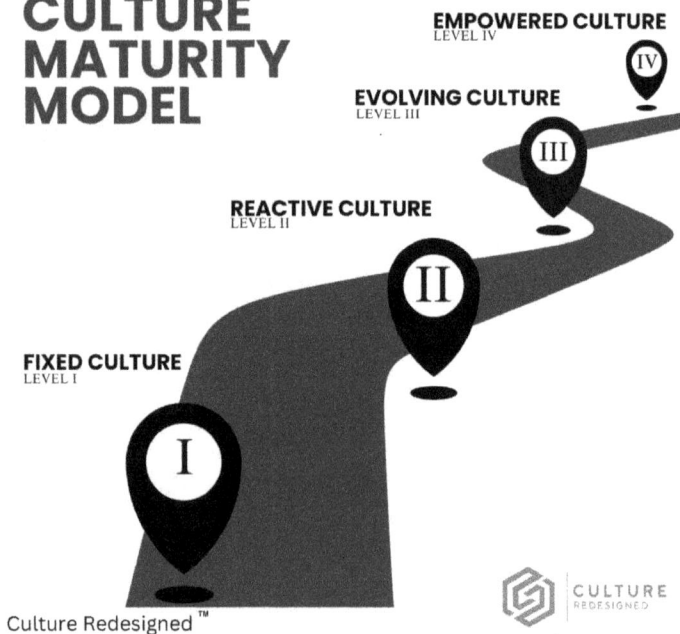

EMPOWERED CULTURE
LEVEL IV

IV

EVOLVING CULTURE
LEVEL III

III

REACTIVE CULTURE
LEVEL II

II

FIXED CULTURE
LEVEL I

I

Culture Redesigned™

CULTURE
REDESIGNED

APPENDIX 2

Evolving From Level I to Level II

	LEVEL I Fixed Culture	LEVEL II Reactive Culture
Culture-Minded Leadership	Leadership's attention to organizational culture is inconsistent and reactionary.	Some leaders display cultural commitment, but it remains limited and uneven.
Shared Values Alignment	Shared values are vaguely defined and displayed.	Shared values are communicated but inconsistently reflected in behavior.
Employee Engagement	Employees have little influence or participation in shaping organizational culture.	Employee engagement is inconsistent and primarily top-down.
Collaboration and Trust	Collaboration is minimal; teams operate in silos with low trust.	Some teams collaborate, but trust and transparency are still lacking across the organization.
Equity and Belonging	Equity and belonging efforts are absent or minimal.	Some equity-driven activities are in place, but they lack depth or widespread impact.
Innovation and Continuous Learning	Innovation is rare, and there are no formal processes for learning or improvement.	Innovation and learning occur in isolated teams with limited organizational impact.

To support this transition, we usually start by creating a Culture Blueprint.

Step-by-Step Process to Complete Deliverable

1. Facilitated meeting with Executive Leadership.
   - Create a culture statement and select 3-5 shared values.
   - Create collective definitions of each value. For example, if the value is abstract, like inclusion or respect, ask the team to share their personal definitions of that value and then create a collective definition that will guide the culture blueprint.

2. Executive leaders facilitate a workshop with an extended leadership team.
   - Communicate the importance of cultivating culture in the organization.
   - Communicate the desire to listen and integrate the teams' input in the creation of a formalized culture blueprint.
   - Present culture statement and defined shared values.
   - Have the team brainstorm to list behaviors that support the modeling of defined shared values as it relates to the work.
   - Create a plan to communicate the culture.

Culture Blueprint Recommendations
   - Include a culture statement and shared values on your website, in waiting rooms, on job postings, etc.

- Incorporate all steps as part of the onboarding process, feedback meetings, conflict resolution, etc.
- Involve leadership, HR, and key cultural influencers in the organization during the creation process.
- Host workshops or brainstorming sessions to align on key components.
- Share drafts for feedback and refine them based on input to ensure buy-in.

Culture Blueprint

Culture Statement: Create a culture statement as if you are describing the experience to a team member.

Defined Shares Values: Create a list of 3-5 shared values, creating a collective definition for each.

-
-
-
-
-

Behavioral Application: List actual behaviors or habits that team members should embrace to demonstrate each of the shared values. Think about employee experience, customer service experience, how they approach the work, how they interact with each other and the community around them.

-
-
-
-

Alignment with Organizational Goals: Describe how your culture statement supports business outcomes such as innovation, collaboration, and engagement.

Culture Blueprint Action Plan

Implementation Steps: Define how the culture will be cultivated (e.g., training, policies, strategies, etc.).

1.
2.
3.
4.
5.

Milestones: Set short-term and long-term goals for culture development.

Short-term goals:

●

●

●

Long-term goals:

●

●

●

Evolving From Level II to Level III

Culture-Minded Leadership	Some leaders display cultural commitment, but it remains limited and uneven.	Leadership consistently communicates and upholds cultural values across the organization.
Shared Values Alignment	Core values are communicated but inconsistently reflected in behavior.	Shared values are widely understood and embedded into key organizational processes.
Employee Engagement	Employee engagement is inconsistent and primarily top-down.	Structured engagement programs exist, encouraging employee input and involvement.
Collaboration and Trust	Some teams collaborate, but trust and transparency are still lacking across the organization.	Collaborative frameworks exist, with an emphasis on fostering trust across teams.
Equity & Belonging	Some equity-driven activities are in place, but they lack depth or widespread impact.	Equity and Inclusion strategies are established, with structured programs across the organization.
Innovation and Continuous Learning	Innovation and learning occur in isolated teams, with limited organizational impact.	Continuous learning and innovation are encouraged through formal programs.
	LEVEL II **Reactive Culture**	**LEVEL III** **Evolving Culture**

Facilitating a Trust Mapping Session to Improve Culture

Trust is the foundation of a strong organizational culture. This is a powerful activity because it combines individual introspective reflection with collective brainstorming. Step-by-Step Guide:

Part I

1. Share the definition and formula for trust

$$\text{Trust} = \frac{(\text{Credibility} + \text{Reliability} + \text{Value Deposits})}{\text{Self-Orientation}}$$

- Credibility: Skills, expertise, and consistency of message.
- Reliability: Following through on commitments.
- Value Deposits: Building authentic relationships.
- Self-Orientation: Prioritizing the team's goals over personal agendas.

Objective: Identify existing trust levels and gaps within teams.

Instructions: Participants map their workplace relationships on a chart with two axes:

- X-axis: Depth of Trust (Low to High)
- Y-axis: Frequency of Interaction (Low to High)

Plot key colleagues or stakeholders on the chart and discuss strategies to improve trust with low-trusted individuals.

Execution:

2. Create the Individual Trust Map (See template)
   - Ask participants to draw a two-axis chart on a sheet.
   - Label the X-axis as Depth of Trust (low trust on the left, high trust on the right).
   - Label the Y-axis as Frequency of Interaction (low interaction at the bottom, high interaction at the top).

3. Identify Key Workplace Relationships
   - Ask participants to think about colleagues or stakeholders they interact with regularly.
   - Focus on relationships that significantly impact their work.

4. Plot Individuals on the Chart
   - Using sticky notes or markers, have each participant place names on their chart based on their perceived level of trust and interaction with each person. This is an individual segment of the session. Participants will be asked to share trends but not names.

5. Analyze the Map
   o Discuss trends
   o Identify individuals who fall in **low-trust zones** and explore possible reasons.
   o Highlight strong trust relationships and the best practices that contribute to them.

Individual Trust Mapping Chart (Template)

	Low Frequency of Interaction	High Frequency of Interaction
High Depth of Trust		
Low Depth of Trust		

Reflection Questions:

- Which quadrant contains the most names?
- What does this indicate about your workplace relationships?
- For individuals in the **Low Trust, High Interaction** quadrant, what specific behaviors are hindering trust?

- How can you leverage relationships in the **High Trust, Low Interaction** quadrant to strengthen your team dynamics?

Part 2

Collective Brainstorming and behavioral chart

1. After individually reflecting on their own trust maps, ask participants to brainstorm behaviors that they should start, stop, or continue. List the behaviors and make sure they align with the shared values. You can use our template.

2. Schedule a follow-up session to review progress

Shared Value	Behavior to Stop	Behavior to Start	Behavior to Continue
Shared Value A			
Shared Value B			
Shared Value C			

APPENDIX 4

Evolving From Level III to Level IV

Culture-Minded Leadership	Leadership consistently communicates and upholds cultural values across the organization.	Leaders demonstrate a continuous, proactive approach to nurturing and evolving culture.
Shared Values Alignment	Shared values are widely understood and embedded into key organizational processes.	Shared values are fully integrated, continuously driving actions and strategies.
Employee Engagement	Structured engagement programs exist, encouraging employee input and involvement.	Employees are deeply engaged, empowered, and take active roles in culture development.
Collaboration and Trust	Collaborative frameworks exist, with an emphasis on fostering trust across teams.	Trust is a cornerstone of the culture, with seamless collaboration across the organization.
Equity & Belonging	Equity and Inclusion strategies are established, with structured programs across the organization.	Equity fully embedded, with a culture of belonging and leadership in diversity practices.
Innovation and Continuous Learning	Continuous learning and innovation are encouraged through formal programs.	Continuous learning and innovation are part of the organizational fabric, with regular feedback loops and improvement efforts.

Level IV Empowered cultures have a built-in continuous improvement effort for each of the six capabilities.

The most common sessions we facilitate to support organizations at this level are listed below:

- Culture Sustainability Session – Our Three-legged Stool below
- Fostering Innovation & Continuous Learning
- Team Collaboration Strategy - improving trust and alignment
- Feedback Loops & Learning Cultures: Building systems for ongoing improvement

CULTURE SUSTAINABILITY THREE LEGGED STOOL

Accountability

Trust

Psychological Safety

Culture Redesigned ™

CULTURE REDESIGNED

APPENDIX 5

Reading List

- *Neuroscience of Inclusion: New Skills for New Times*, Mary E. Casey and Shannon Murphy
- *Radical Respect: How to Work Together Better*, Kim Scott
- *The Waymakers: Clearing the Path to Workplace Equity with Competence and Confidence,* Tara Jaye Frank
- *The Includers: The 7 Traits of Culturally Savvy, Anti-Racist Leaders*, Colette A.M. Phillips
- *The Science of Dream Teams: How Talent Optimization Can Drive Engagement, Performance, and Happiness*, Mike Zani
- *The Speed of Trust: The One Thing That Changes Everything*, Stephen Covey
- *The Idea-Driven Organization: Unlocking the Power in Bottom-Up Ideas*, Alan G. Robinson and Dean M. Schroeder
- *The Advantage: Why Organizational Health Trumps Everything Else in Business*, Patrick M. Lencioni

BIBLIOGRAPHY

Almaiman, Sulaiman and Dr. Patrick McLaughlin. Facilitating a Continuous Improvement Culture: a Literature Review. *Advances in Transdisciplinary Engineering*, Vol. 8, 2018. https://dspace.lib.cranfield.ac.uk/bitstream/handle/1826/13732/Facilitating_a_continuous_improvement_culture-2018.pdf

Casey, Mary E. *Neuroscience of Inclusion: New Skills for New Times.* Outskirts Press, 2017.

Council of State Governments Justice Center Staff. "Researchers Examine Effects of a Criminal Record on Prospects for Employment." CSG Justice Center, 23 September 2014. https://csgjusticecenter.org/2014/09/23/researchers-examine-effects-of-a-criminal-record-on-prospects-for-employment/.

Bakker, A. B., & Demerouti, E. "Towards a Model of Work Engagement." Career Development International 13, no. 3, 2008: 209-223. https://www.emerald.com/insight/content/doi/10.1108/13620430810870476/full/html.

Blanding, Michael. " Collaborating Across Cultures." Harvard Business School, 2012. https://www.library.hbs.edu/working-knowledge/collaborating-across-cultures.

Covey, Stephen. *The Speed of Trust.* New York: Free Press, 2006.

"Culture Is How Employees' Hearts and Stomachs Feel About Monday Morning On Sunday   Night." Employ Humanity, accessed 20 November 2024, https://www.employhumanity.com/culture-is-how-employees-hearts-and-stomachs-feel-about-monday-morning-on-sunday-night-bill-mar.

Decker, S. H., Spohn, C., Ortiz, N. R., & Hedberg, E. "Criminal Stigma, Race, Gender, and Employment: An Expanded Assessment of the Consequences of Imprisonment for Employment." *National Institute of Justice,* 2014.

Ewenstein, Boris, Wesley Smith, and Ashvin Sologar. "Changing Change Management." McKinsey & Company, 1 July 2015. https://www.mckinsey.com/featured-insights/leadership/changing-change-management.

Freeman, L., & Stewart, H. "Toward a Harm-Based Account of Microaggressions." *Perspectives on Psychological Science,* 16(5), 2021: 1008-1023.
        https://doi.org/10.1177/17456916211017099.

Frost, Natasha A., Carlos E. Monteiro, Jacob I. Stowell, Jessica Trapassi, and Stacie St. Louis. " The Impact of Correction Officer Suicide on the Institutional Environment and on the Wellbeing of Correctional Employees." National Criminal Justice Reference Service, April 2021. https://www.ojp.gov/pdffiles1/nij/grants/300715.pdf.

Gallup, Inc. "State of the Global Workplace Report." Gallup.com, 11 November 2024. https://www.gallup.com/workplace/349484/state-of-the-global-workplace.aspx?thank-you-report-form=1.

Gelles, David. "Billionaire No More: Patagonia Founder Gives Away the Company." The New York Times, 14 September 22. https://www.nytimes.com/2022/09/14/climate/patagonia-climate-philanthropy-chouinard.html.

Great Place to Work®. "HubSpot." Great Place to Work®, January 2024. https://www.greatplacetowork.com/certified-company/1298970.

Guidara, Will. *Unreasonable Hospitality: The Remarkable Power of Giving People More Than They Expect.* New York: Optimism Press, 2022.

Hefti, Jacques and Jonathan Levie. "Entrepreneurial Leadership—Vision Casting and the Role of Signalling." Kidmore End: Academic Conferences International Limited, International Conference on Management, Leadership & Governance. 2015: 95-102.

Kaizen Institute. "Building a Continuous Improvement Culture." Kaizen Institute, accessed 21 January 2025. https://kaizen.com/insights/continuous-improvement-culture/.

Müller, R., J. Geraldi, and J. R. Turner. "Relationships Between Leadership and Success in

Different Types of Project Complexities." *IEEE Transactions on Engineering Management*, vol. 59, no. 1, Feb. 2012: pp. 77-90. https://ieeexplore.ieee.org/document/5730485.

Murphy, Mary C. *Cultures of Growth*. New York: Simon & Schuster, 2024.

National Partnership for Women & Families. "Addressing the Latina Wage Gap." National Partnership for Women & Families, 2022. https://www.nationalpartnership.org/our-work/resources/economic-justice/fair-pay/latinas-wage-gap.pdf.

NIJ Staff. "Research on the Mounting Problem of Correctional Officer Stress." *Corrections Today*, November/December 2023. https://www.aca.org/common/Uploaded%20files/Publications_Carla/Docs/Corrections%20Today/2023%20Articles/CT_Nov-Dec_2023_NIJ%20Update.pdf.

Perry, Tyler, director. 2024. *The Six Triple Eight*. Tyler Perry Studios. 2 hrs., 7 min. https://www.netflix.com/title/81590591.

Rozovsky, Julia. "The five keys to a successful Google team." *Rework with Google*, Google, 2015. https://www.michigan.gov/-/media/Project/Websites/mdhhs/Folder4/Folder10/Folder3/Folder110/Folder2/Folder210/Folder1/Folder310/Google-and-Psychological-
        Safety.pdf?rev=7786b2b9ade041e78828f839eccc8b75.

Schmidt, April. "Impactful Employee Engagement Statistics." TWI Institute, accessed 15 January 2025. https://www.twi-institute.com/employee-engagement-statistics/.

Scott, Kim. *Radical Candor: Be a Kick-Ass Boss Without Losing Your Humanity.* New York: St. Martin's Press, 2017.

"Sense of Belonging." Cornell University Diversity and Inclusion, accessed 21 December 2024.https://diversity.cornell.edu/belonging/sense-belonging

Sinek, Simon. *Start With Why: How Great Leaders Inspire Everyone to Take Action.* New York: Portfolio, 2009. https://simonsinek.com/

U.S. Department of Health and Human Services. *Our Epidemic of Loneliness and Isolation: The U.S. Surgeon General's Advisory on the Healing Effects of Social Connection and Community.* U.S. Department of Health and Human Services, 2023. https://www.hhs.gov/sites/default/files/surgeon-general-social-connection-advisory.pdf.

ACKNOWLEDGEMENTS

I could not have written this book without:

- the brilliant directness, unwavering guidance, patience, and belief in my voice, from JoAnna Novak, who helped bring my vision to life with clarity and heart.
- the encouraging support and strategic wisdom of Sara Connell.
- the fascinating, data-driven brain of Dr. Lori Lindbergh, who translated my thoughts into a comprehensive organizational culture and change management assessment.
- the artistry and precision of David Echavarria creating a stunning visual representation of the Culture Maturity Wheel.
- the gift of faith from my mom Zully Moreno, and my late stepdad Ricardo Rey.
- the love and support of Nicholas Rodriguez and Matthew Vaccaro.

ENDORSEMENTS

"Culture-Minded is a must read for anyone leading a team in today's market. In the vein of Simon Sinek and Brene Brown, Vaccaro delivers an important message not just about company culture, but about the betterment of humanity."

- Sara Connell bestselling author of The Science of Getting Rich for Women

" it is said that demographics is destiny. No-where is that phrase more relevant than to businesses and organizations as it relates to their employee hiring needs. Culture – Minded provides the blueprint and six tools for employers in how to create a welcoming and dynamic environment that makes employees feel valued and part of a supportive team. Adriana Vaccaro's lifelong work in this area will benefit any leader who wants to build a positive culture. Culture-Minded is a must read."

-Timothy P. Murray President and CEO Worcester Regional Chamber of Commerce – former LT. Governor of MA

"Culture-Minded is both a philosophy and a framework for what I see as regenerative leadership! The kind of leadership that includes the wellbeing and development of all, while being intentional about building the culture where everything happens. I am excited for this guide that was created with mind and heart to support us, leaders, in the important and complex work of building positive cultures where we can all flourish"

Clara Angelina Diaz-Anderson, founder ClaraFying Coaching and Consulting Institute and Harvard Leadership Instructor.

ABOUT THE AUTHOR

Adriana Vaccaro is the founder and CEO of Culture Rede-signed, a data-driven culture and change management consulting company. With a deep expertise in people analytics, organizational behavior, and leadership development, Adriana helps businesses build high-performance cultures that drive engagement, innovation, and sustainable growth. She was born in Colombia and currently lives in Massachusetts with her husband and three sons.

www.ingramcontent.com/pod-product-compliance
Lightning Source LLC
Chambersburg PA
CBHW060931220326
41597CB00020BA/3515